I0465596

Hope's Adult Coloring Book

By Hope Forster

Copyright © 2018 Arlen Holmgren

All rights reserved. No part of this book may be reproduced or transmitted in any form by any means, electronic or mechanical, including photocopying, scanning and recording or by any information storage and retrieval system, without permission in writing from the publisher, except for the review for inclusion in a magazine, newspaper or broadcast.

Color Pallet

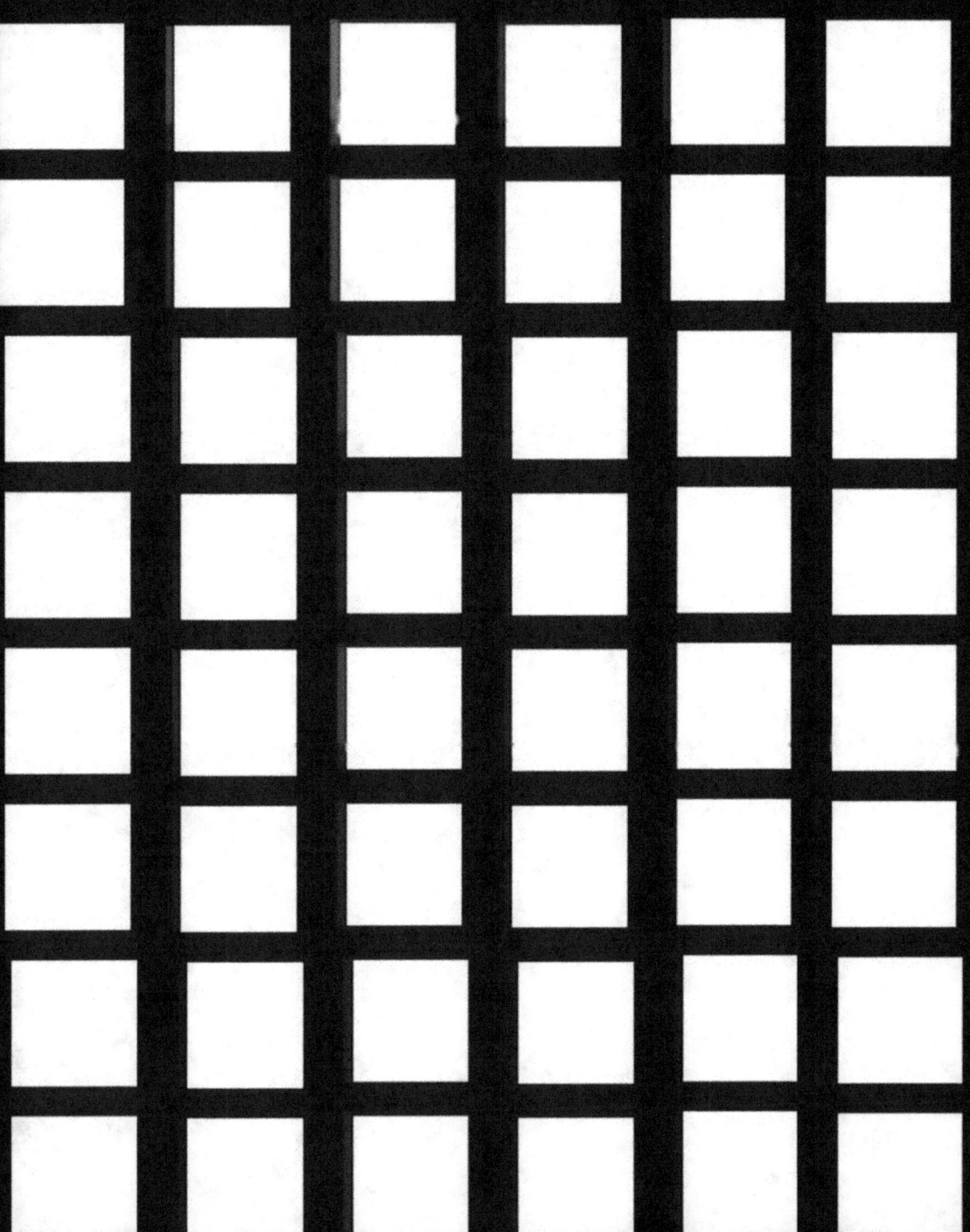

Color Pallet

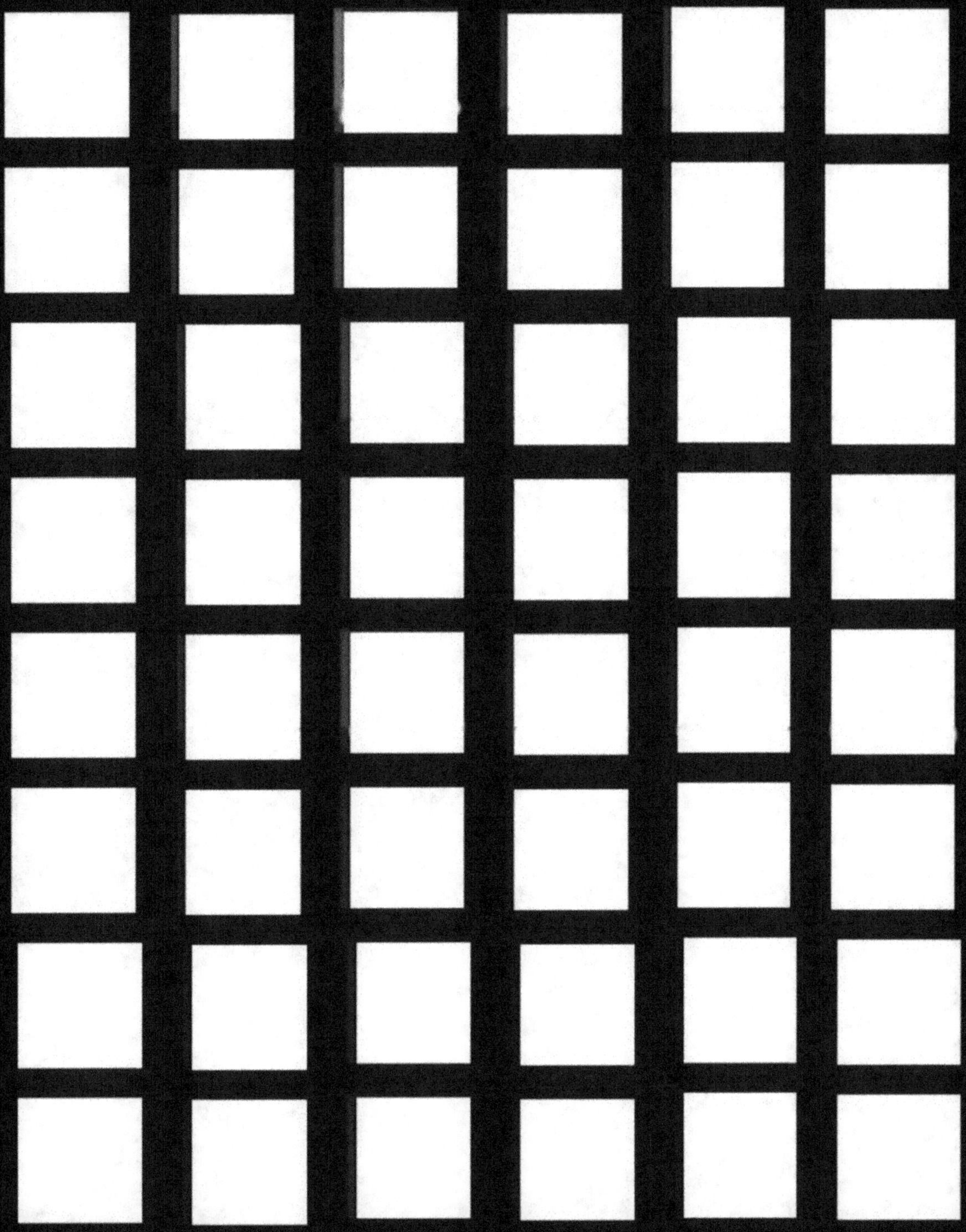

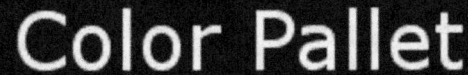

Color Pallet

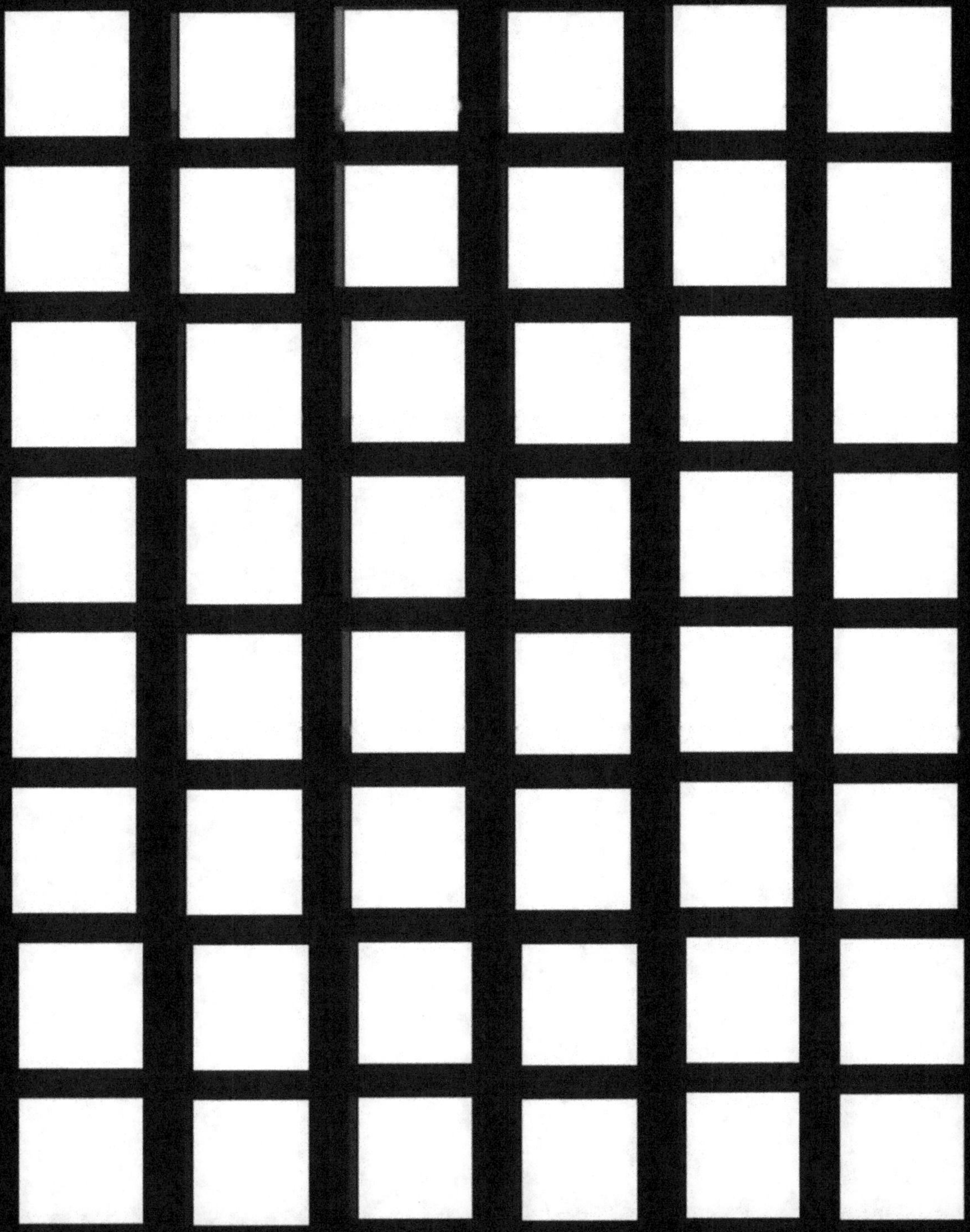

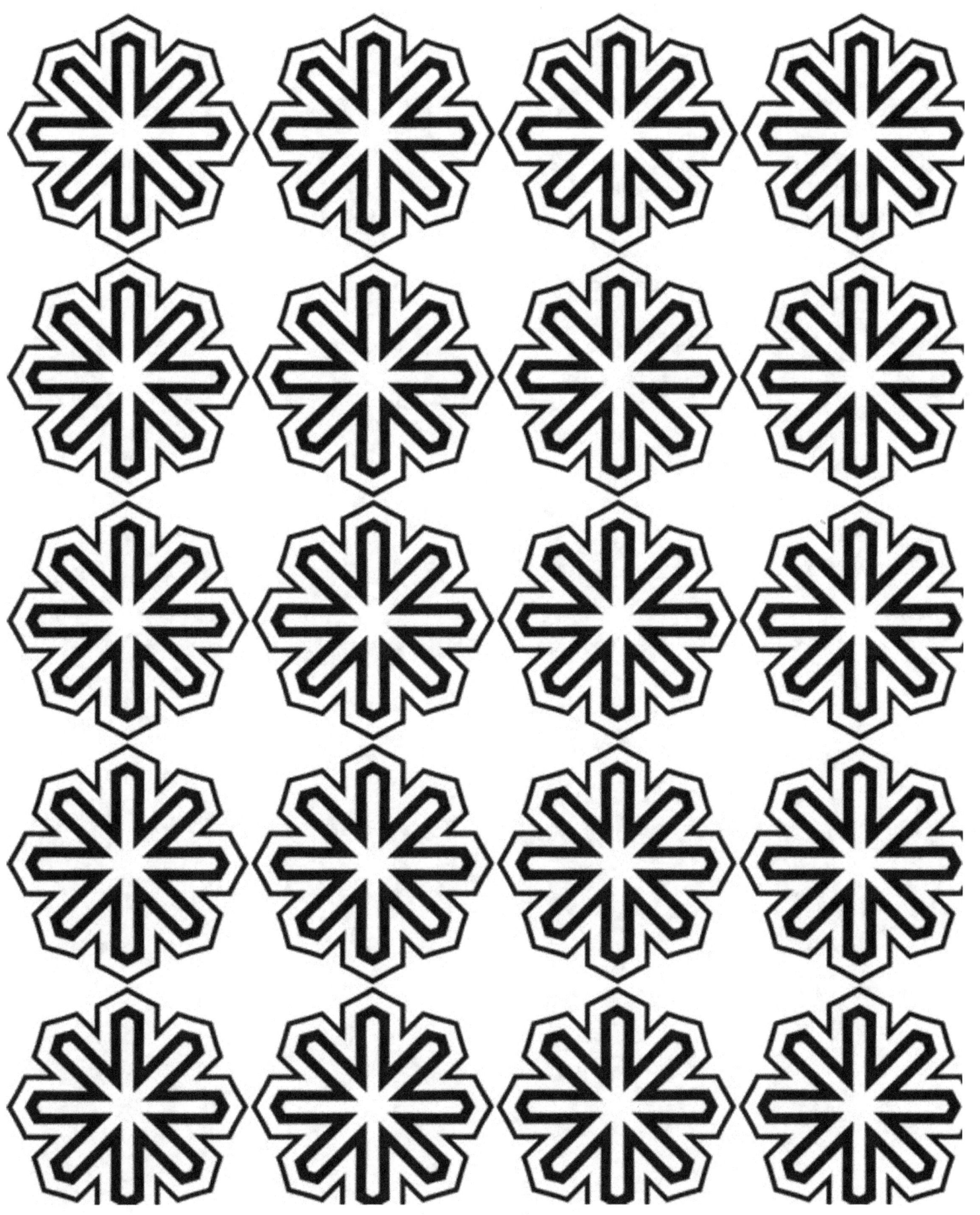

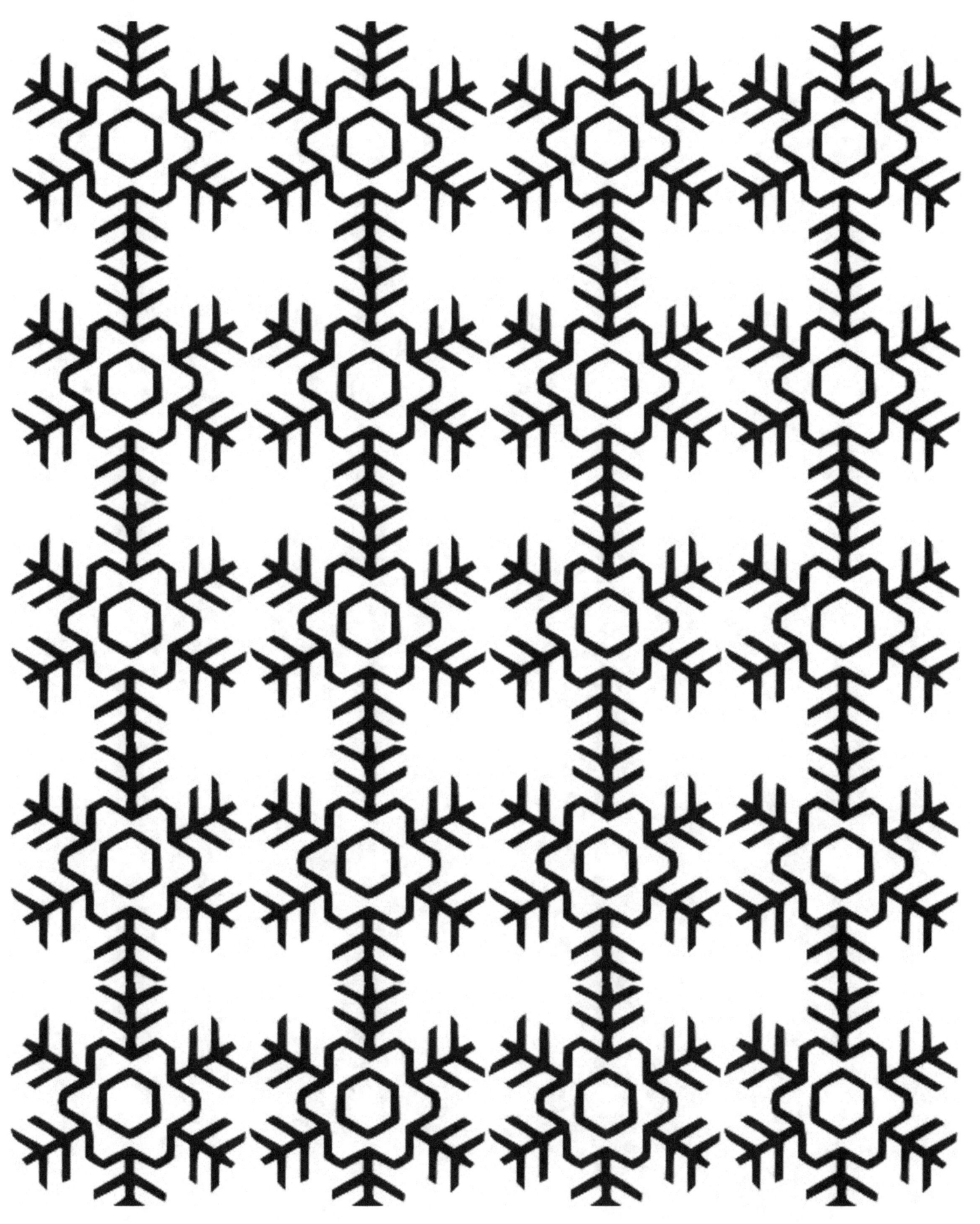

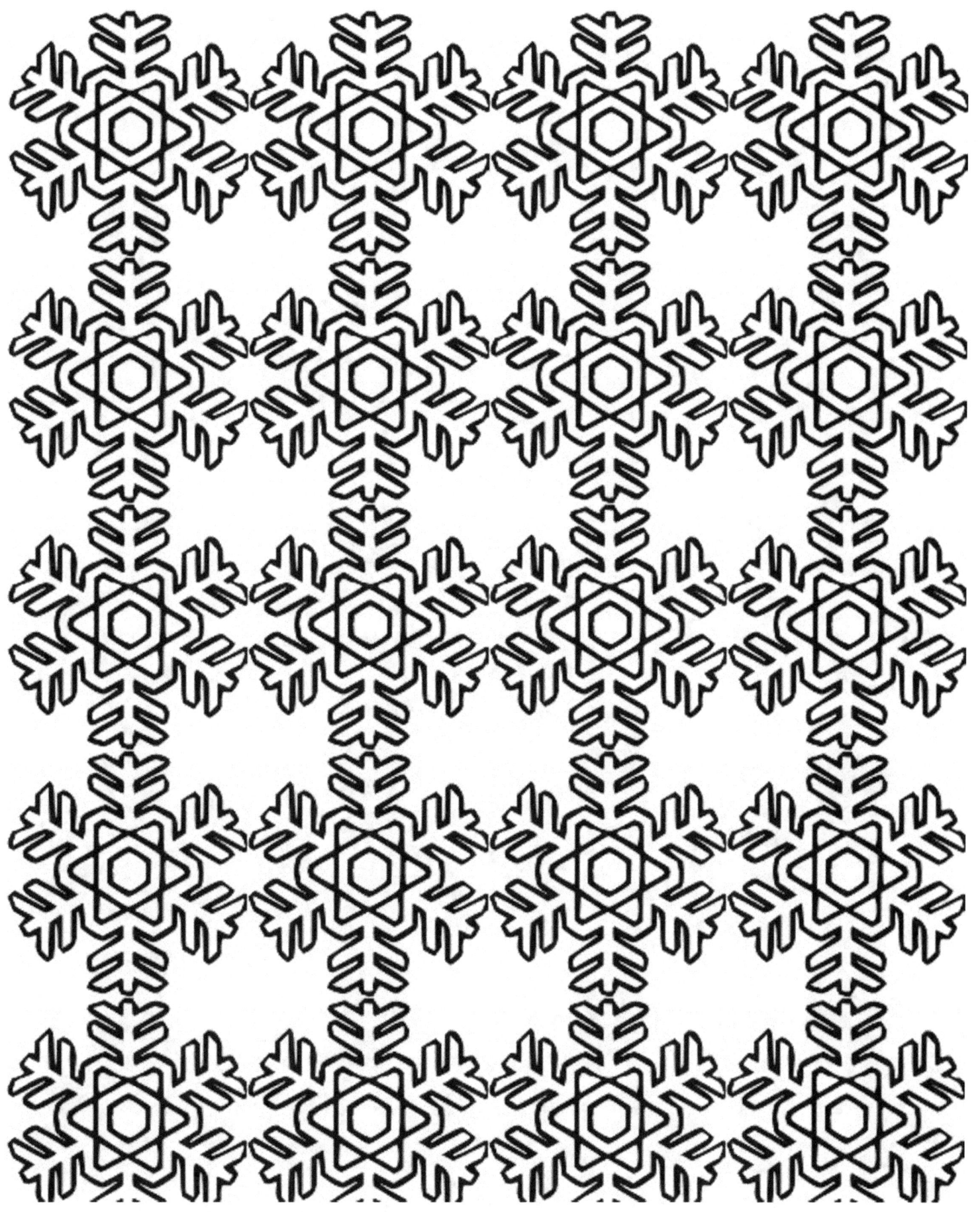

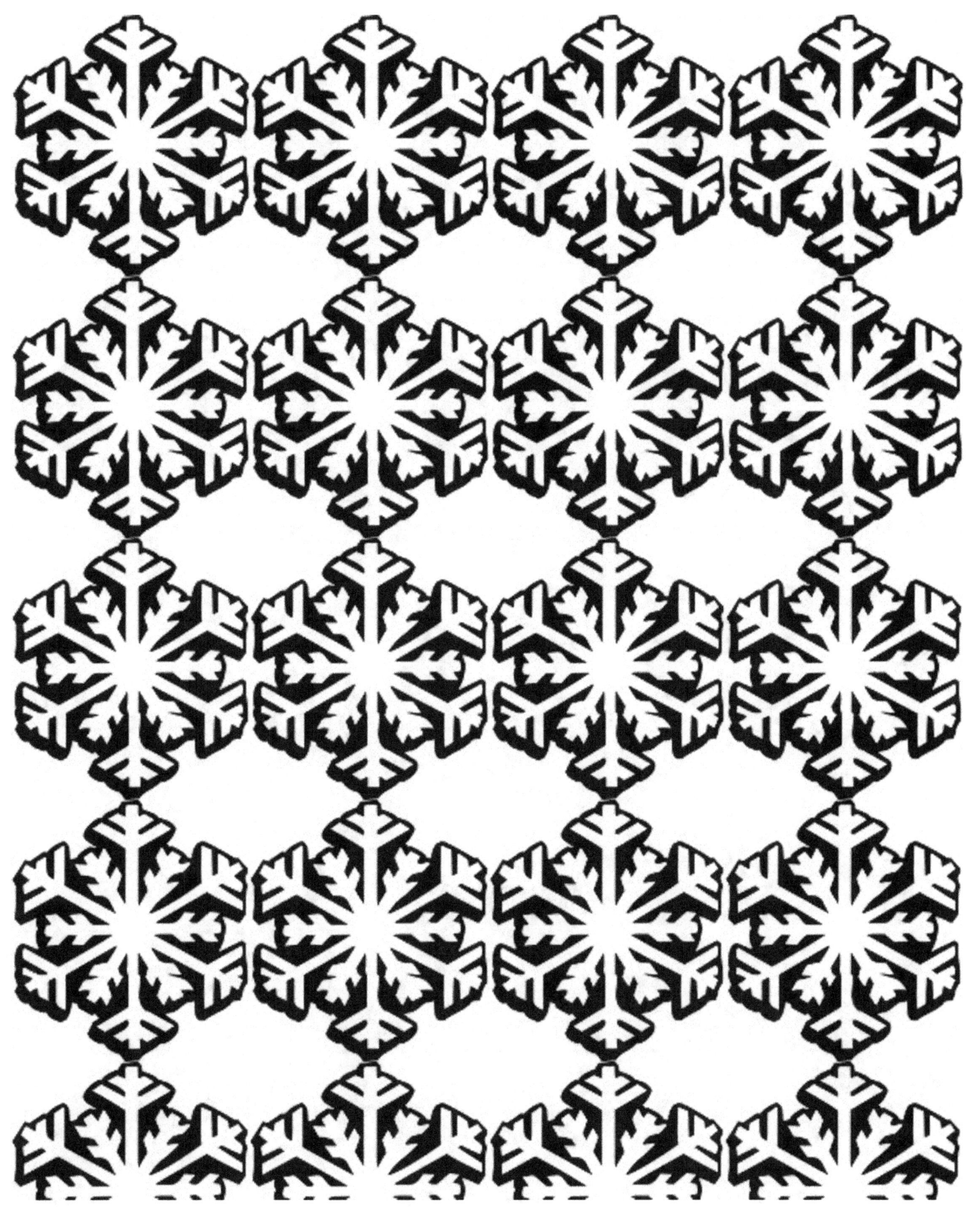

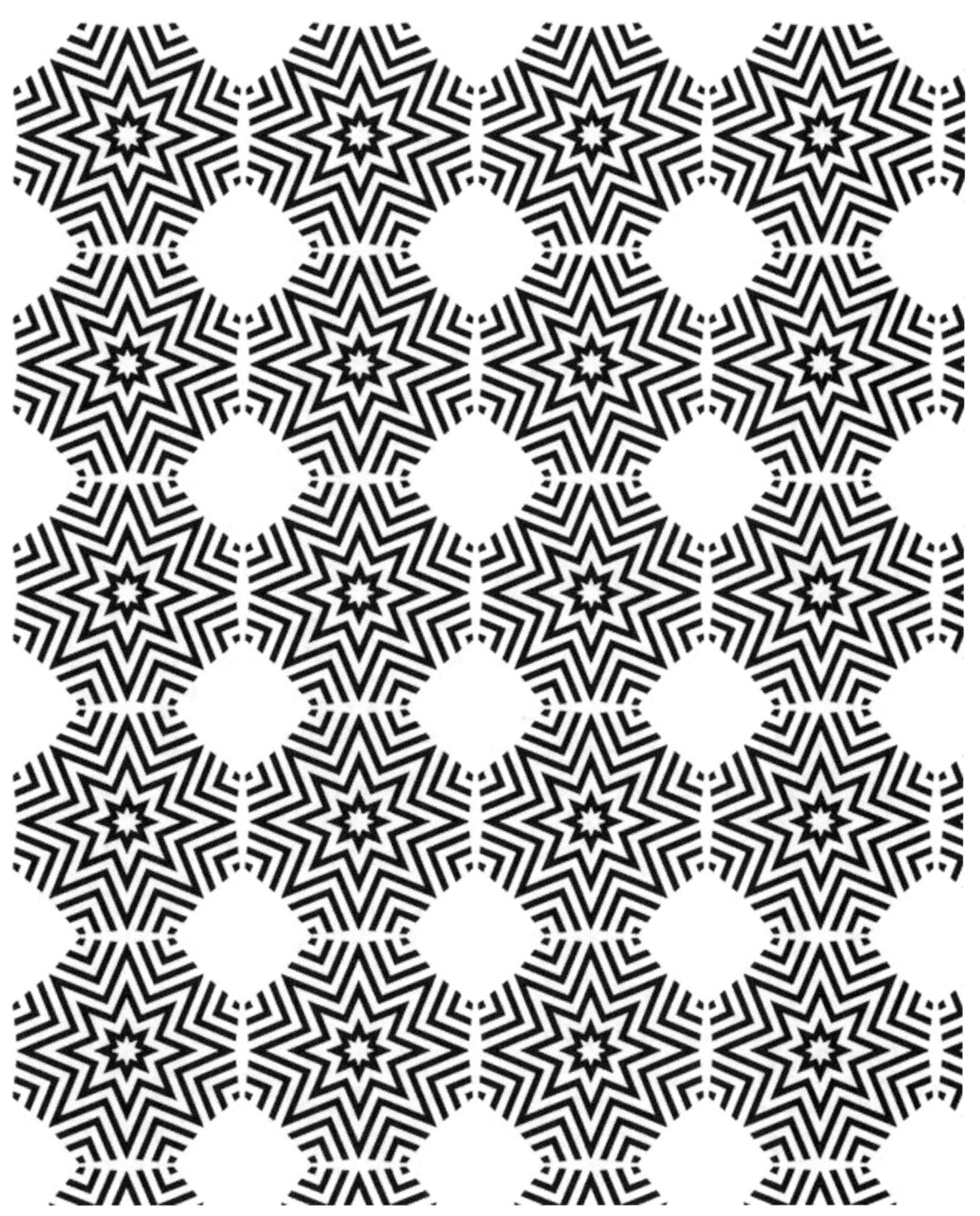

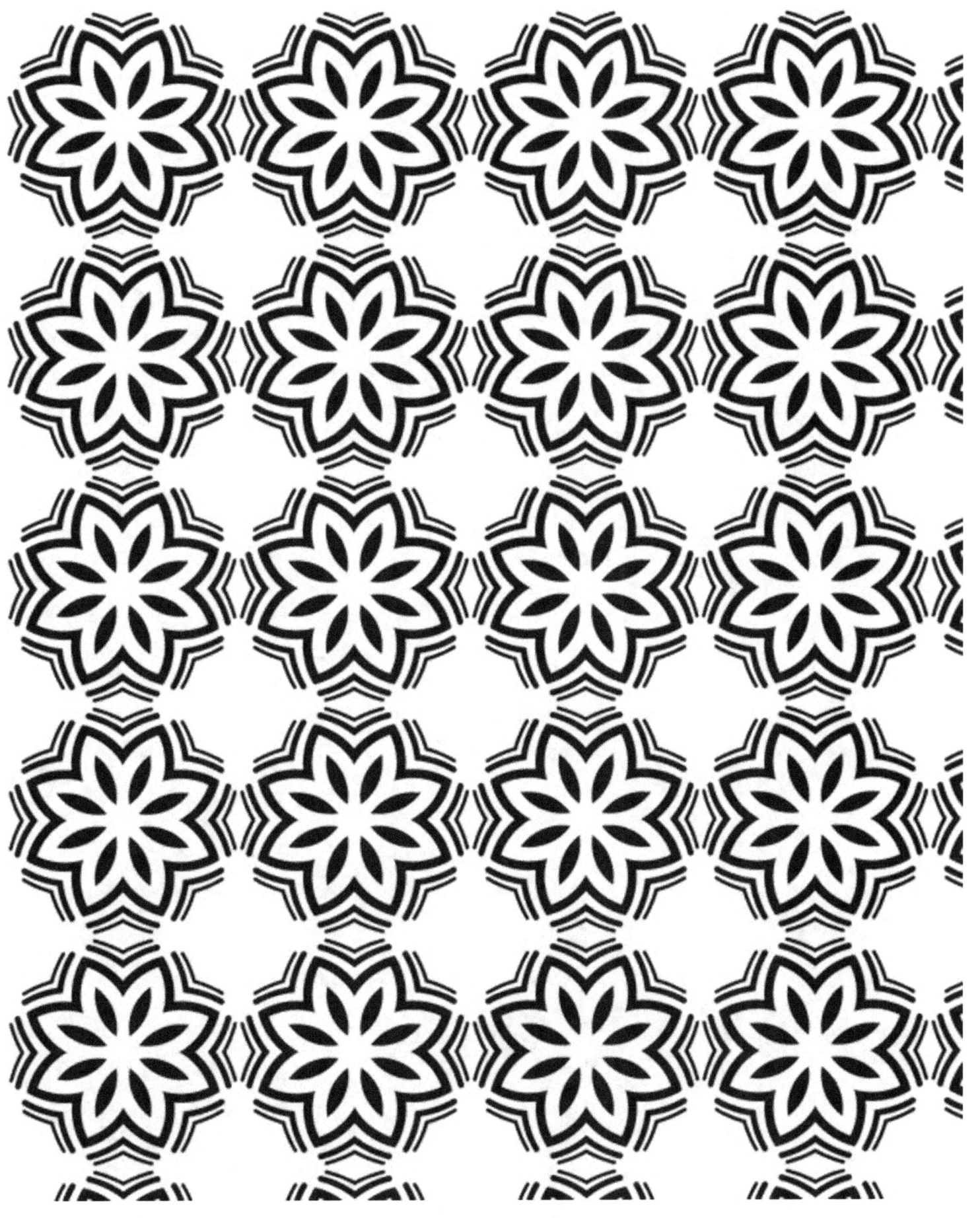

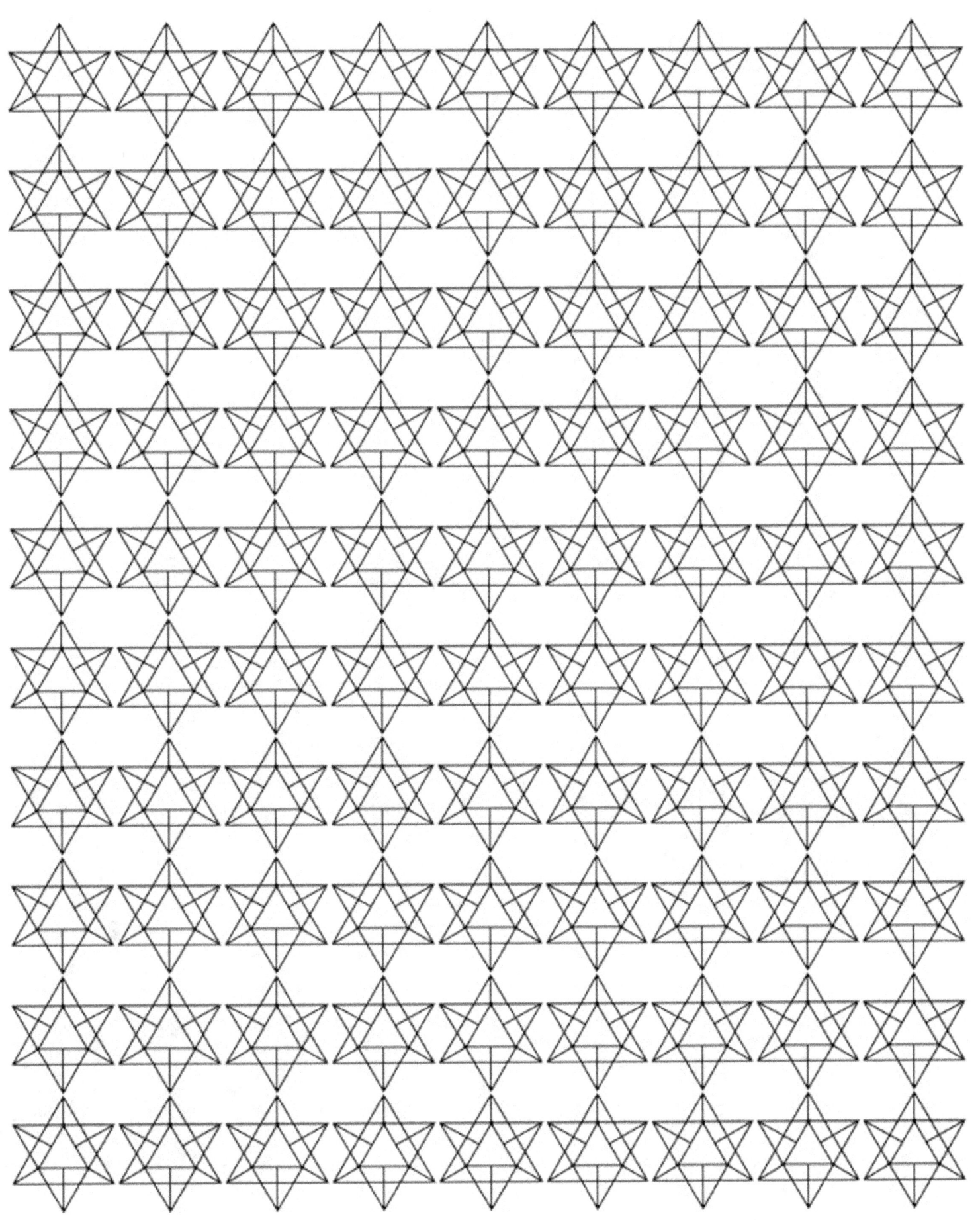

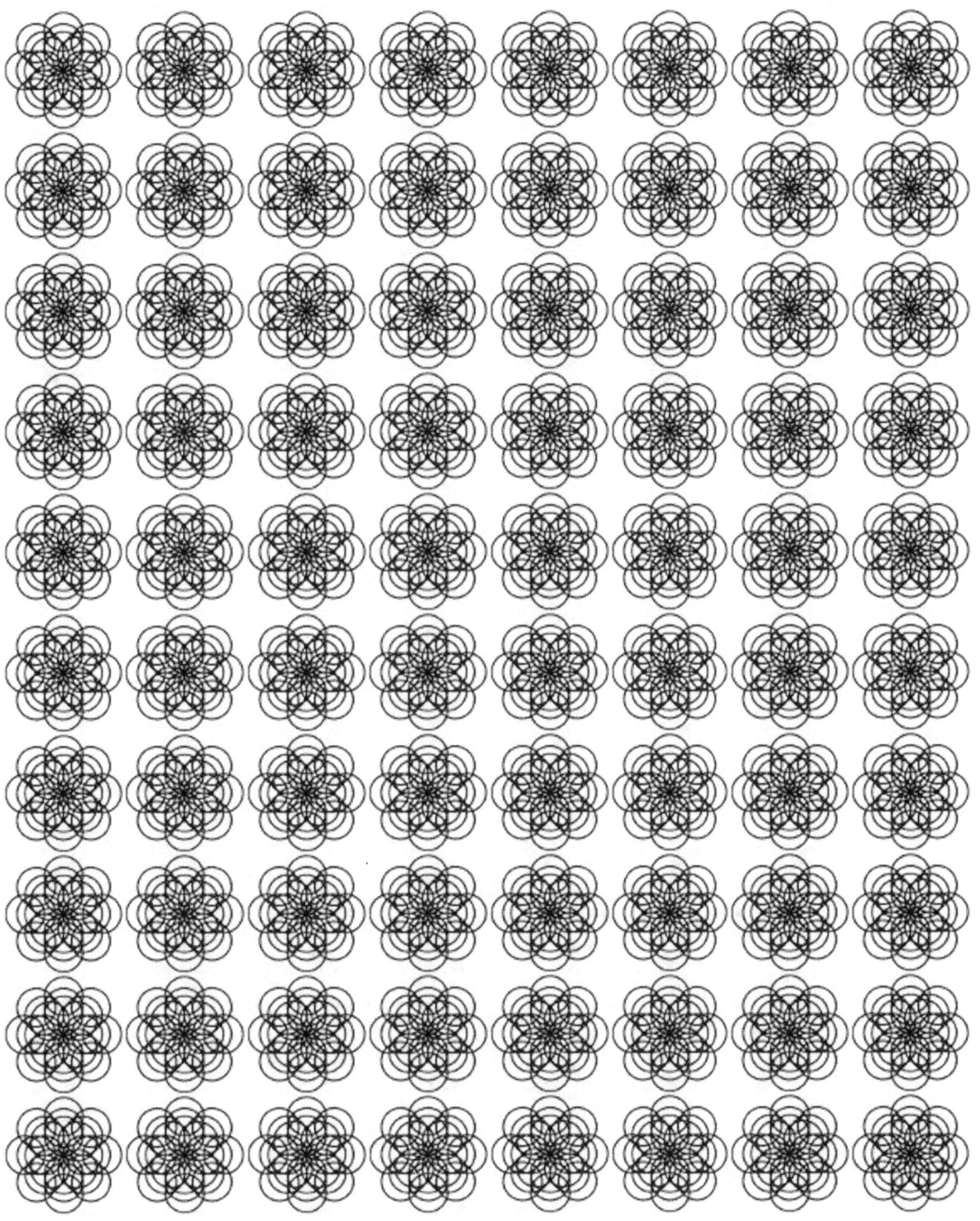

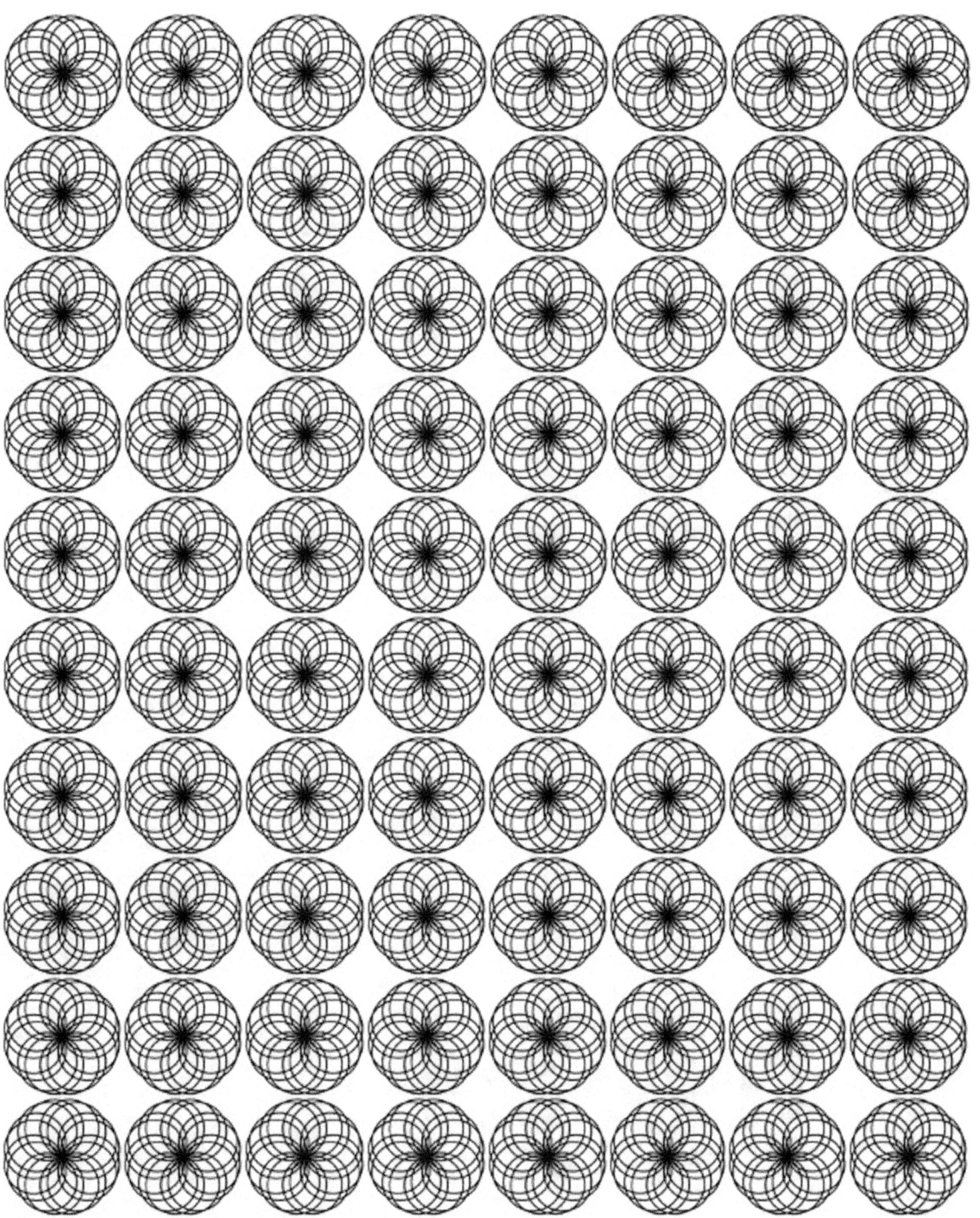

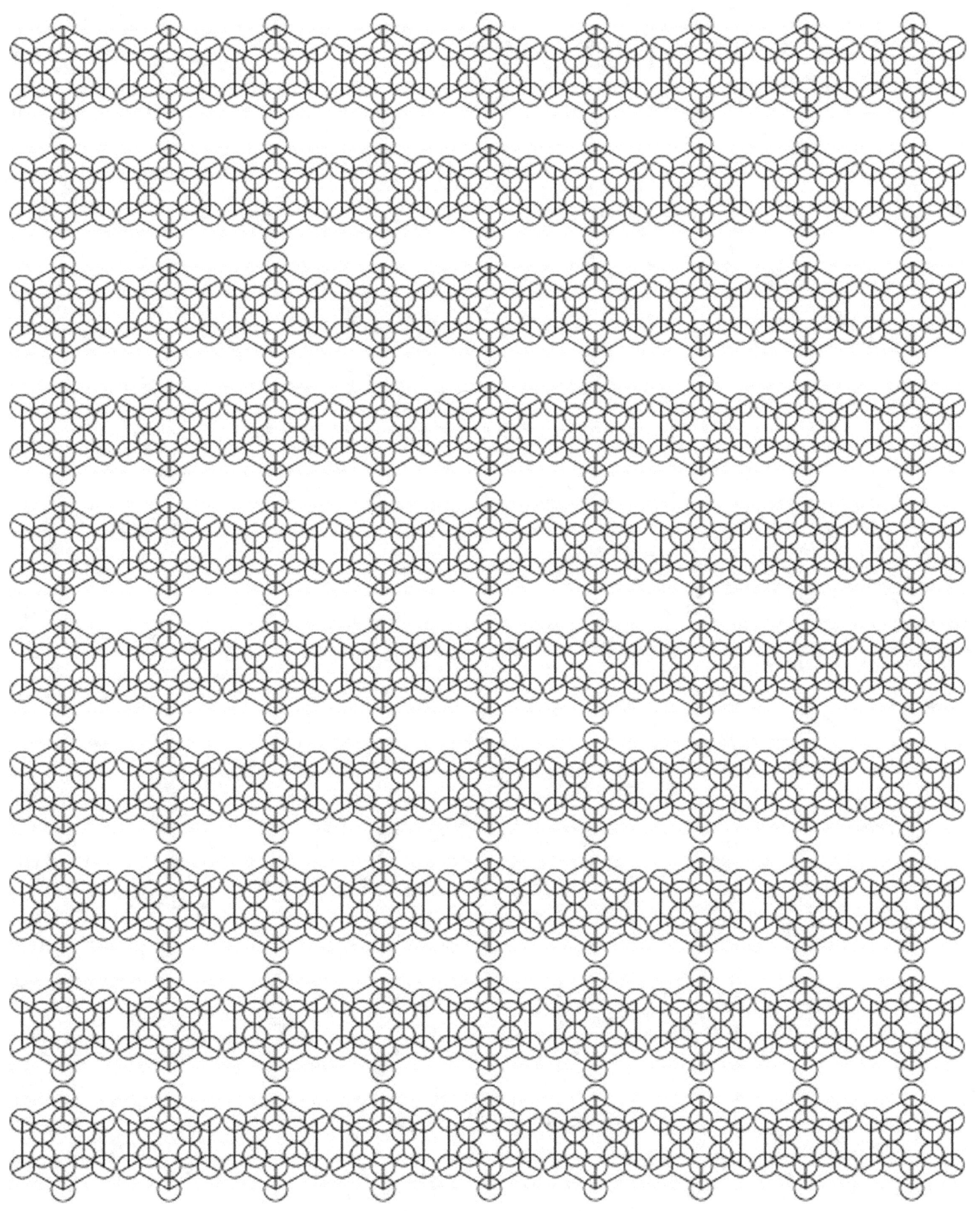

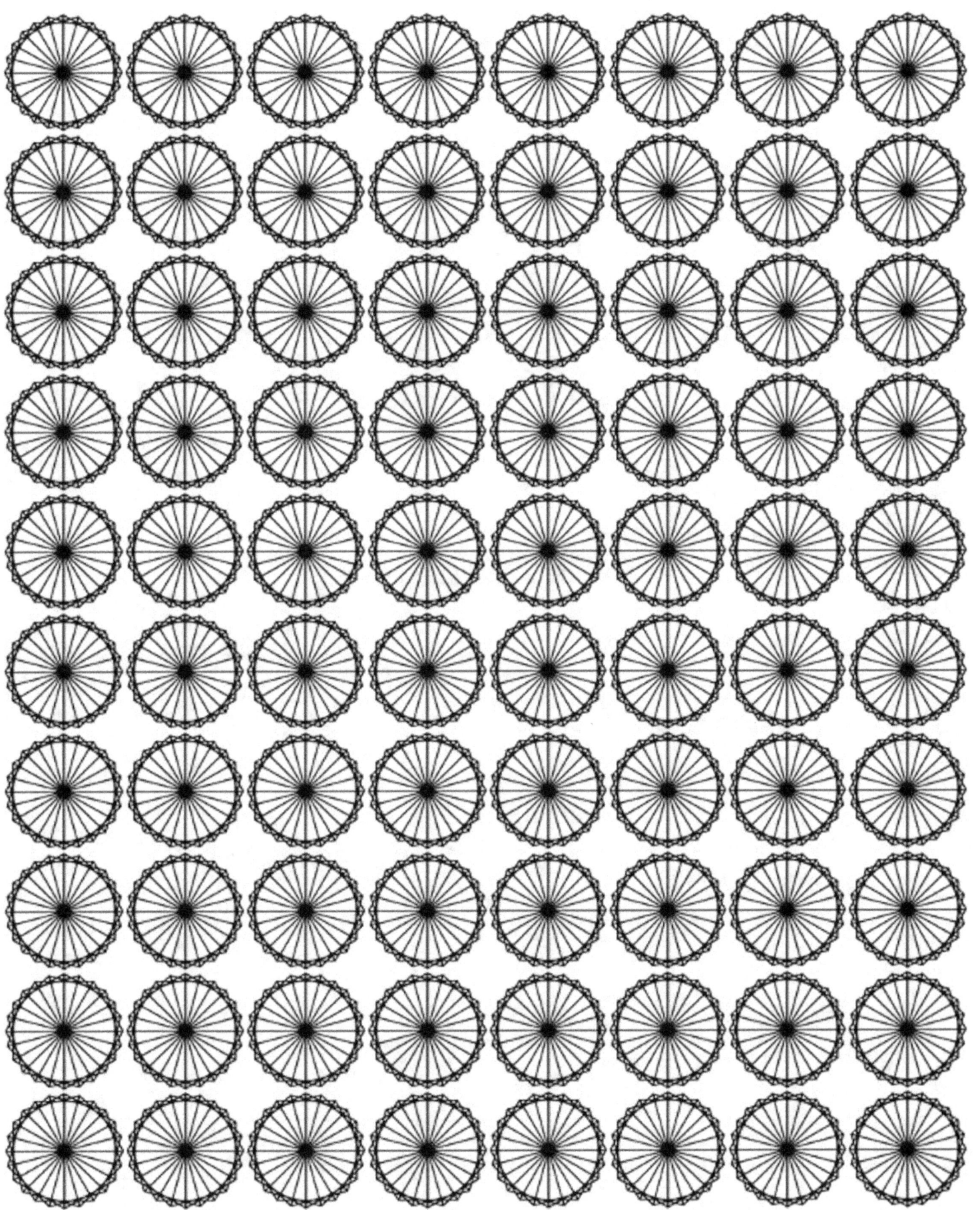

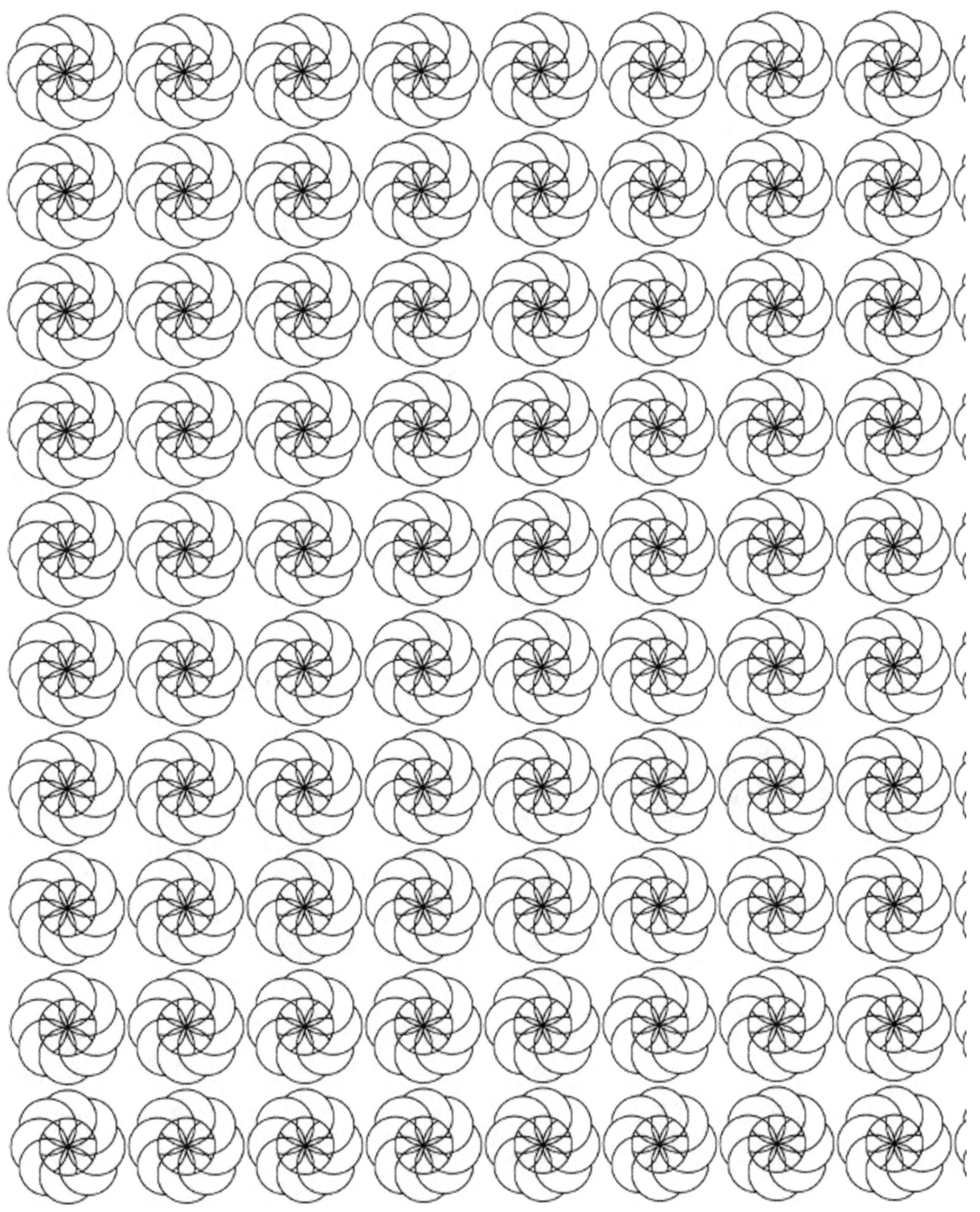

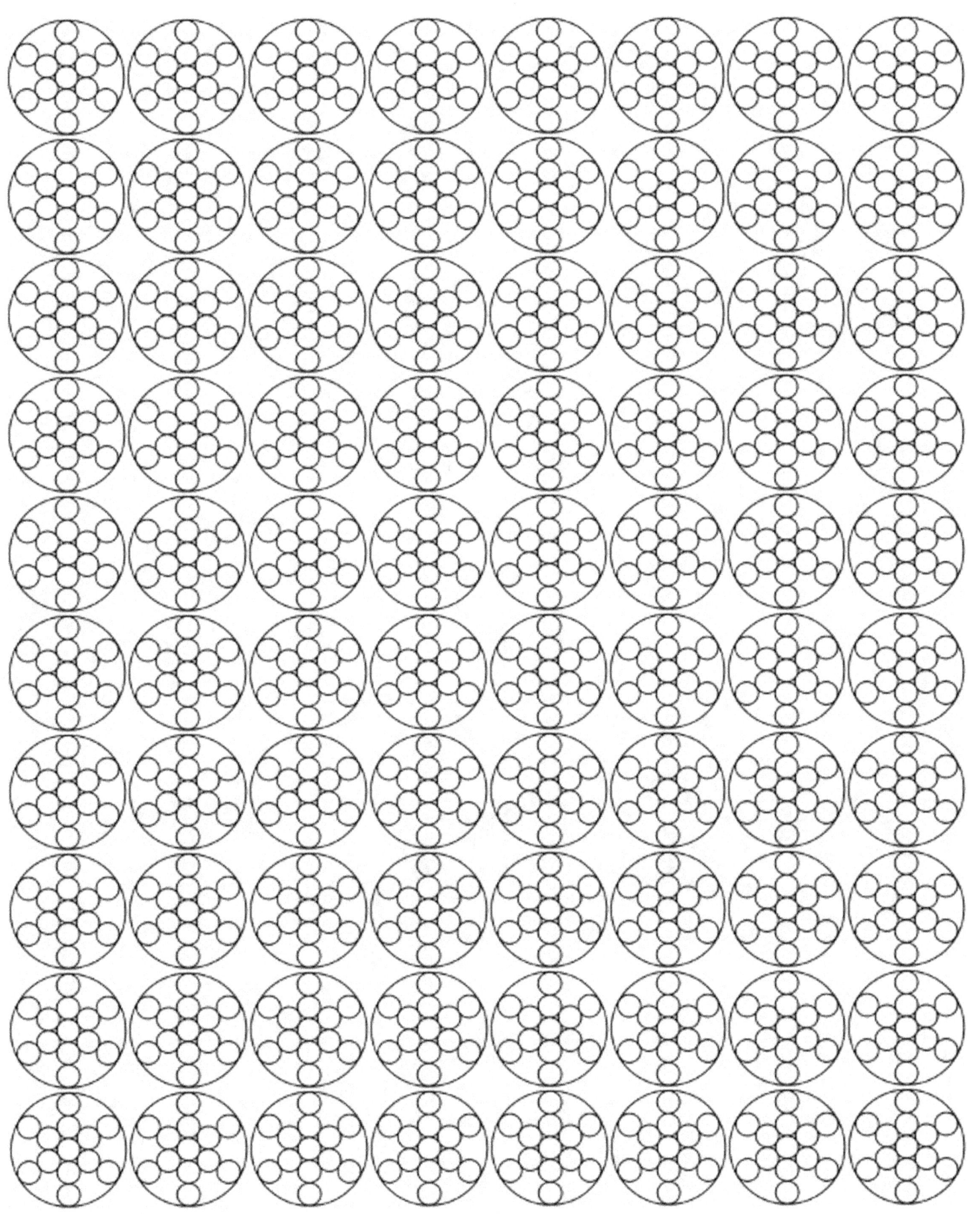

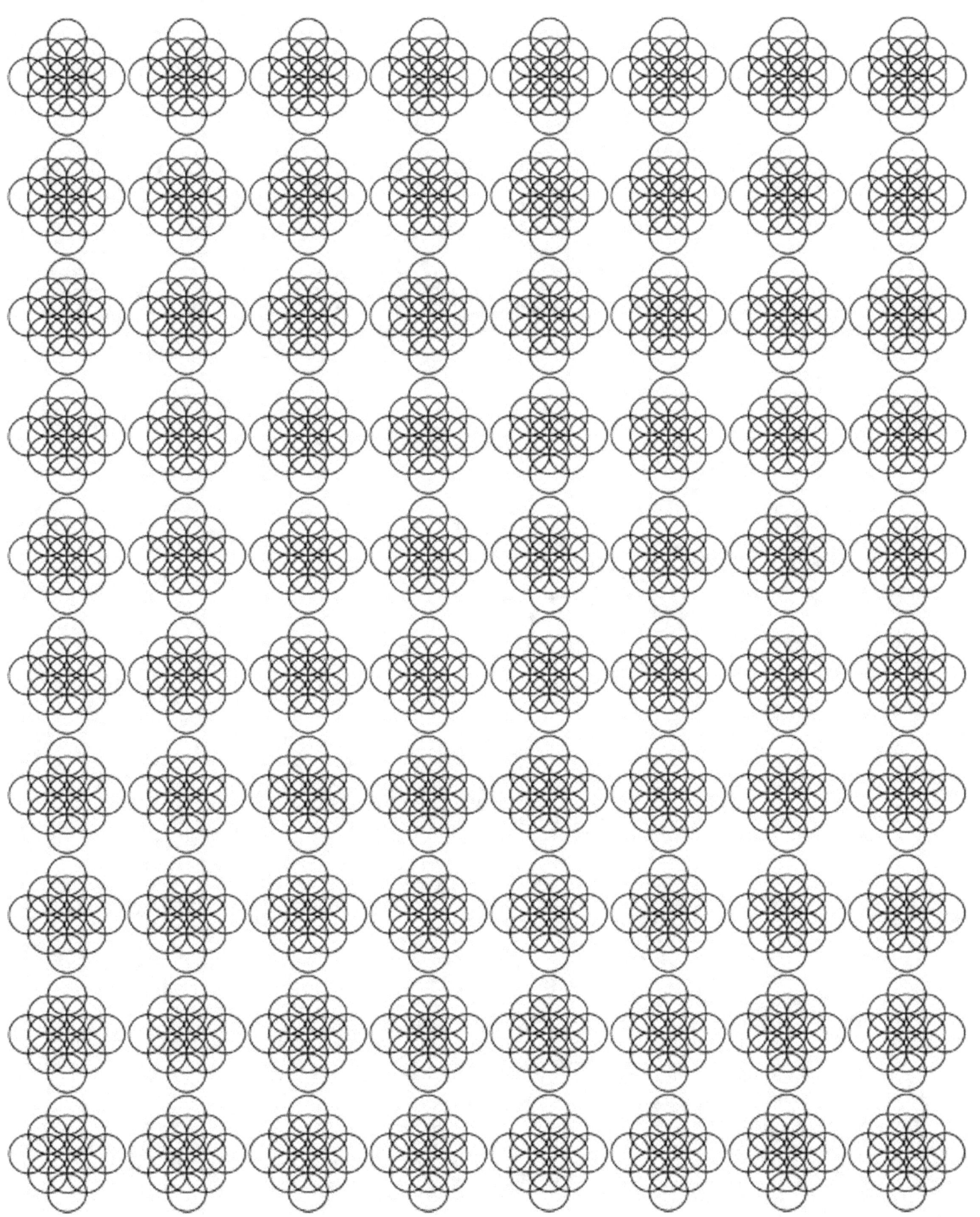

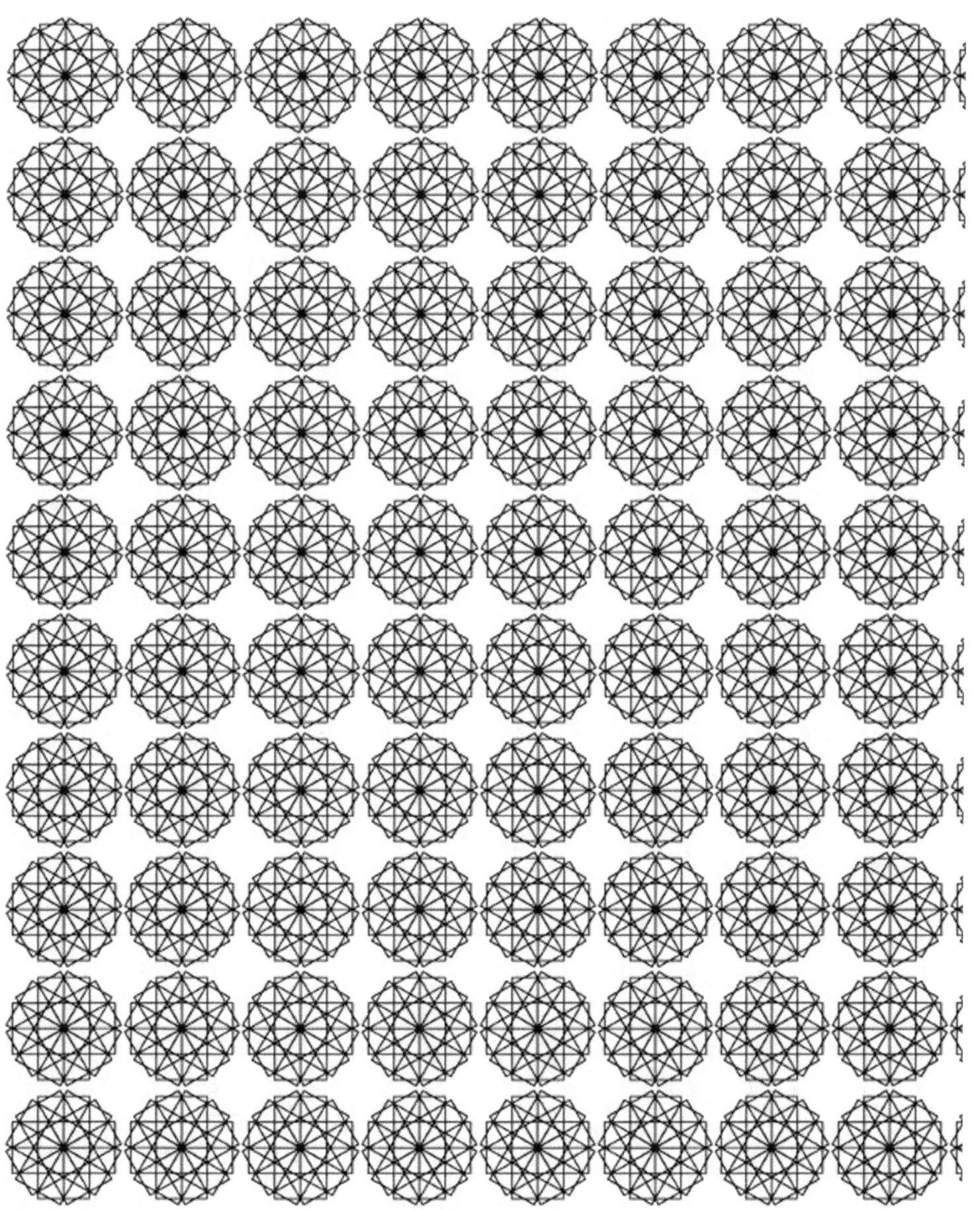

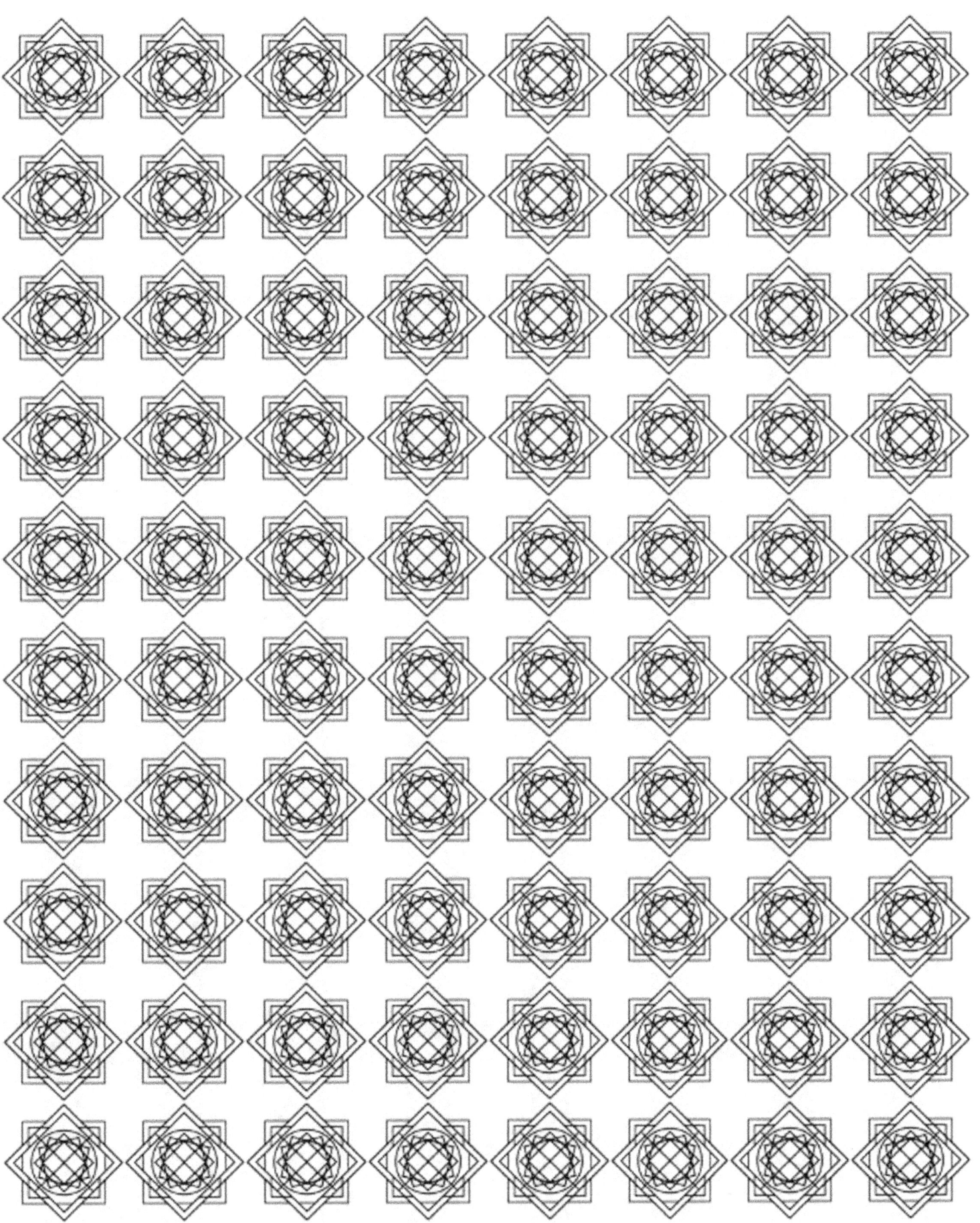

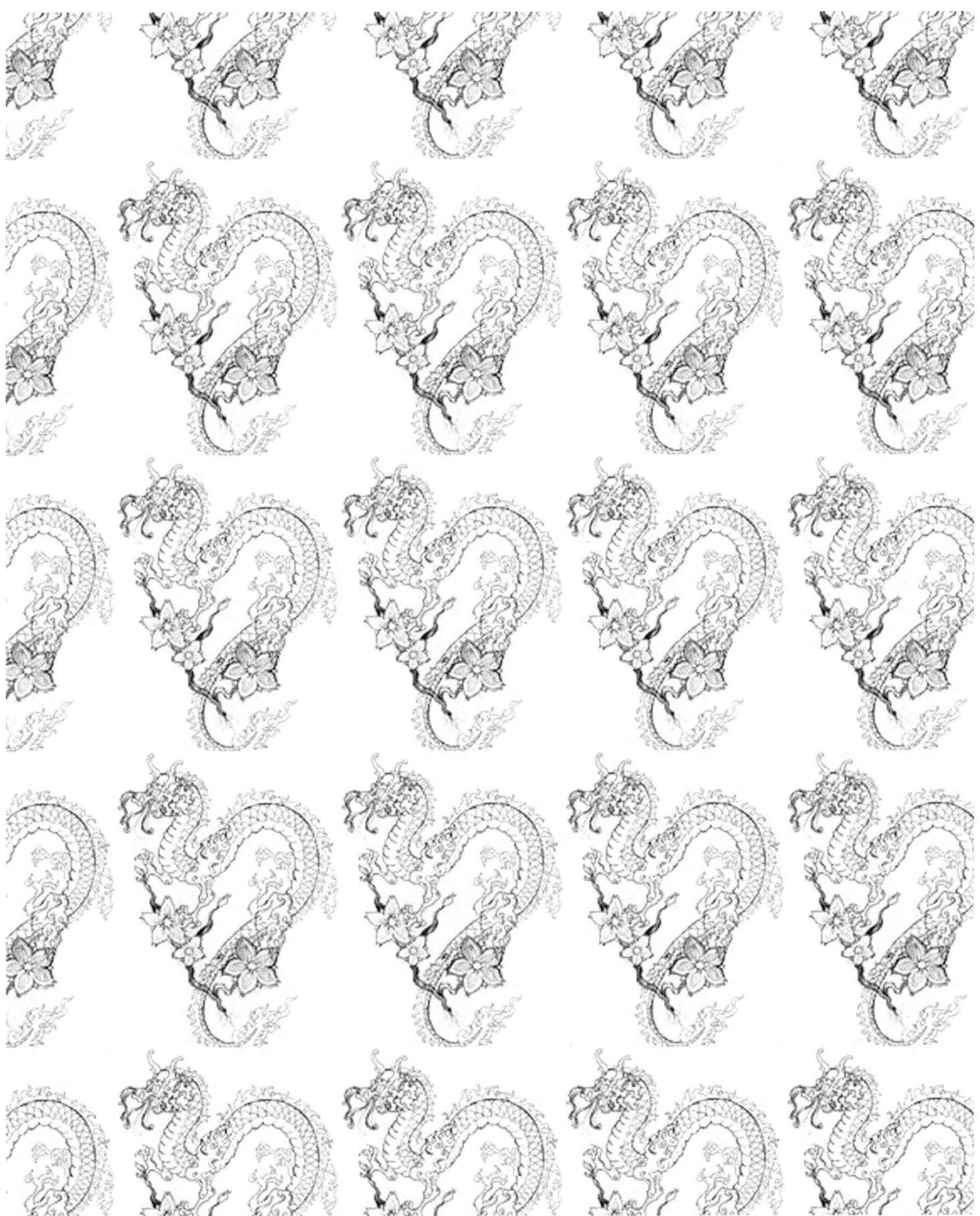

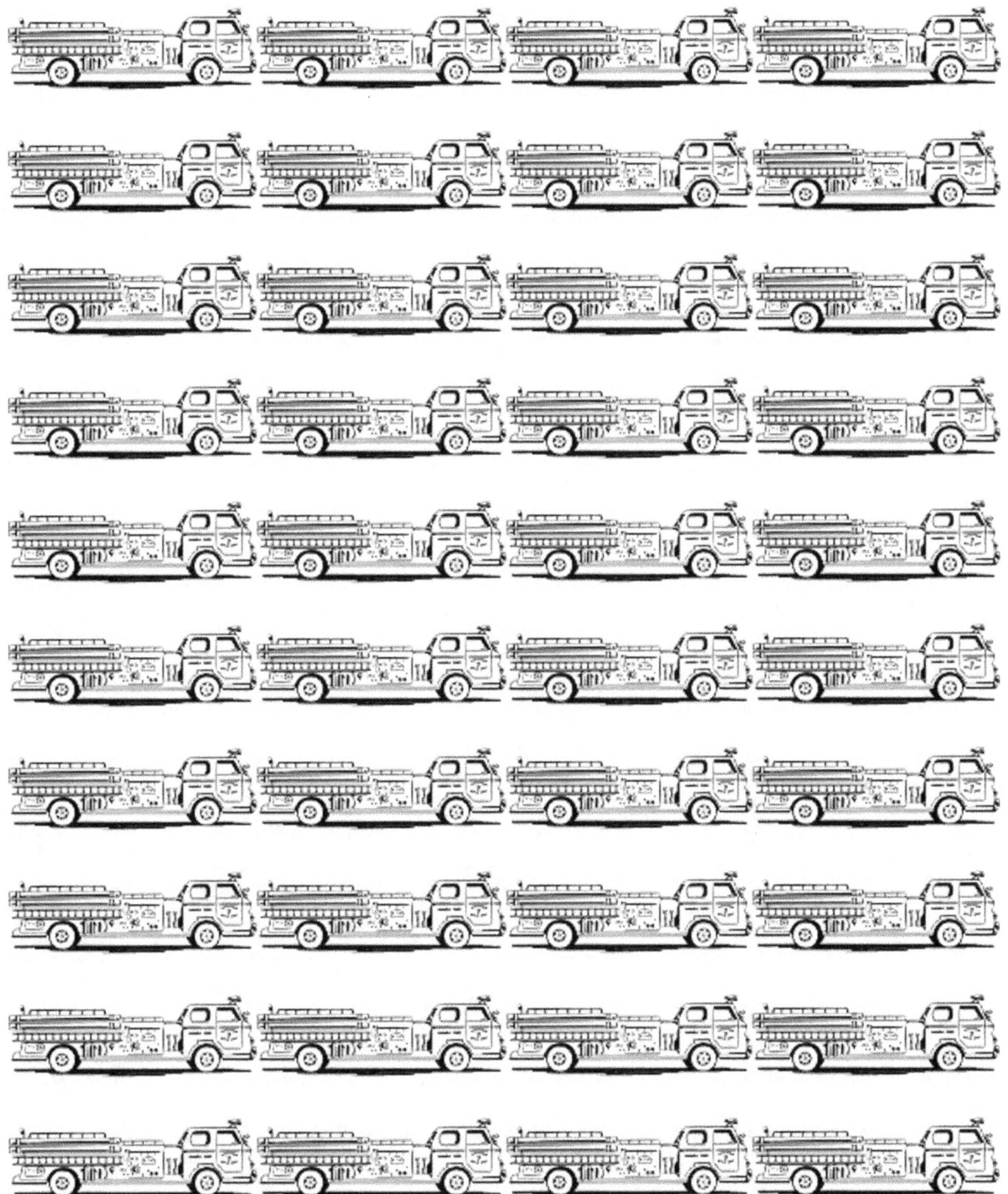

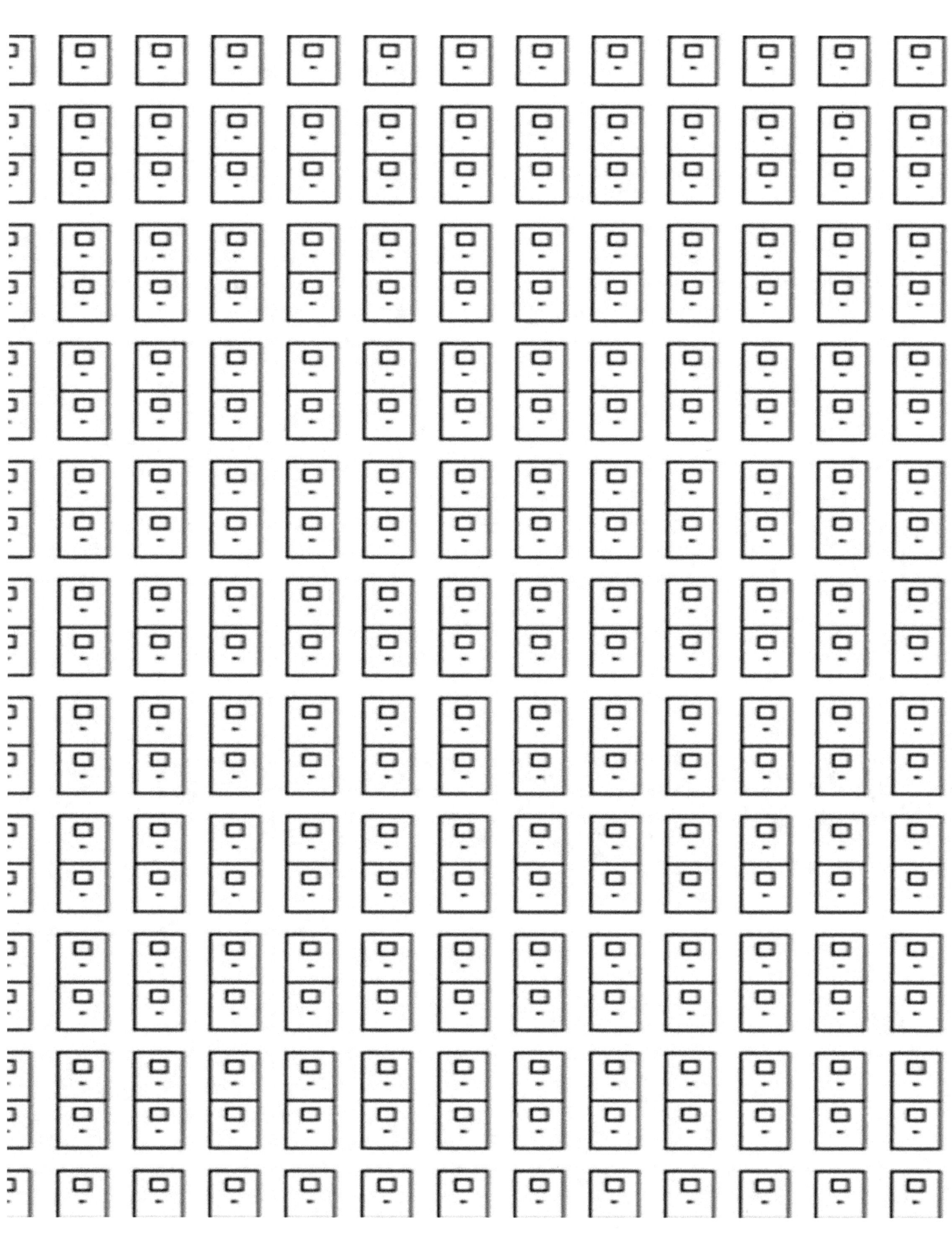

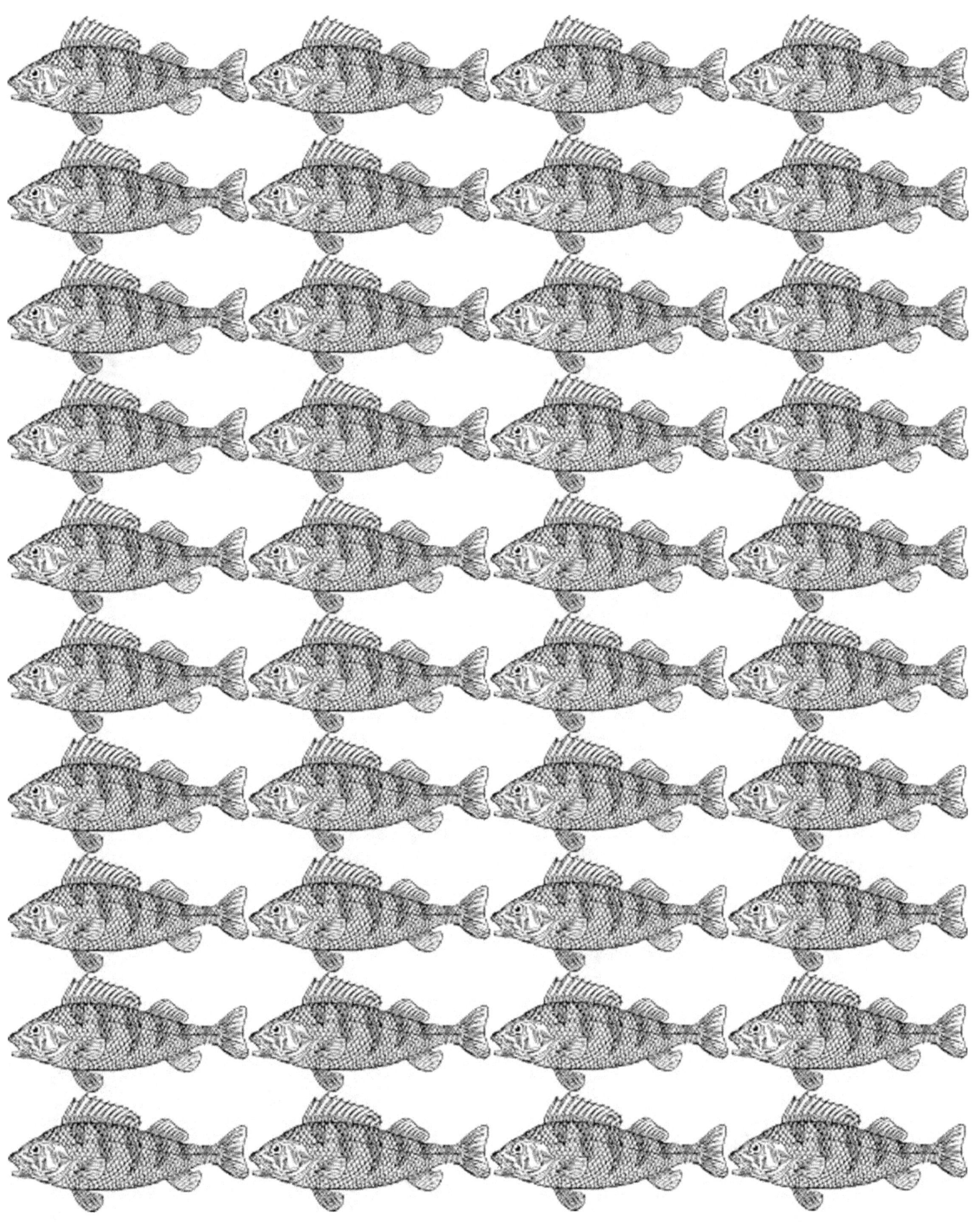

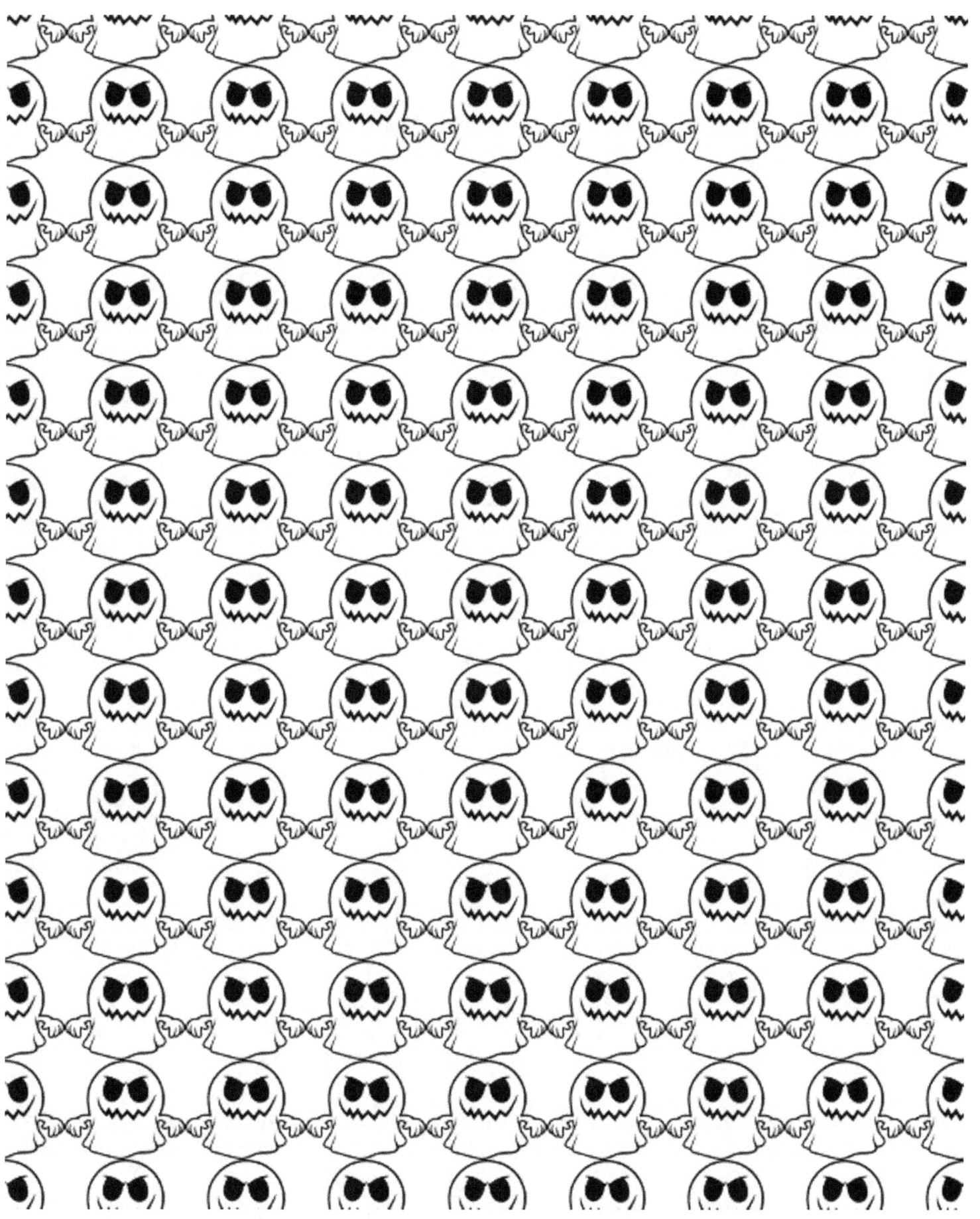

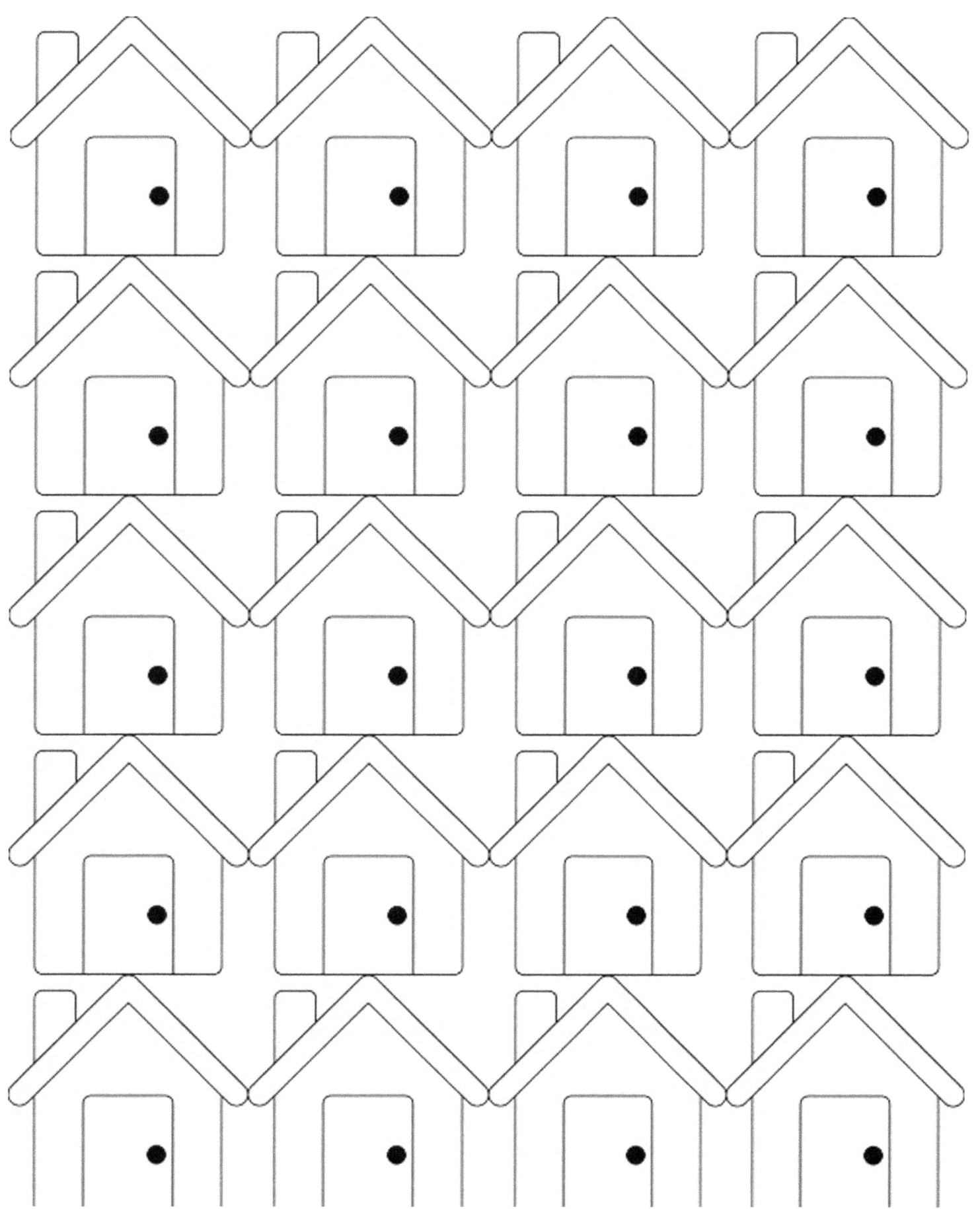

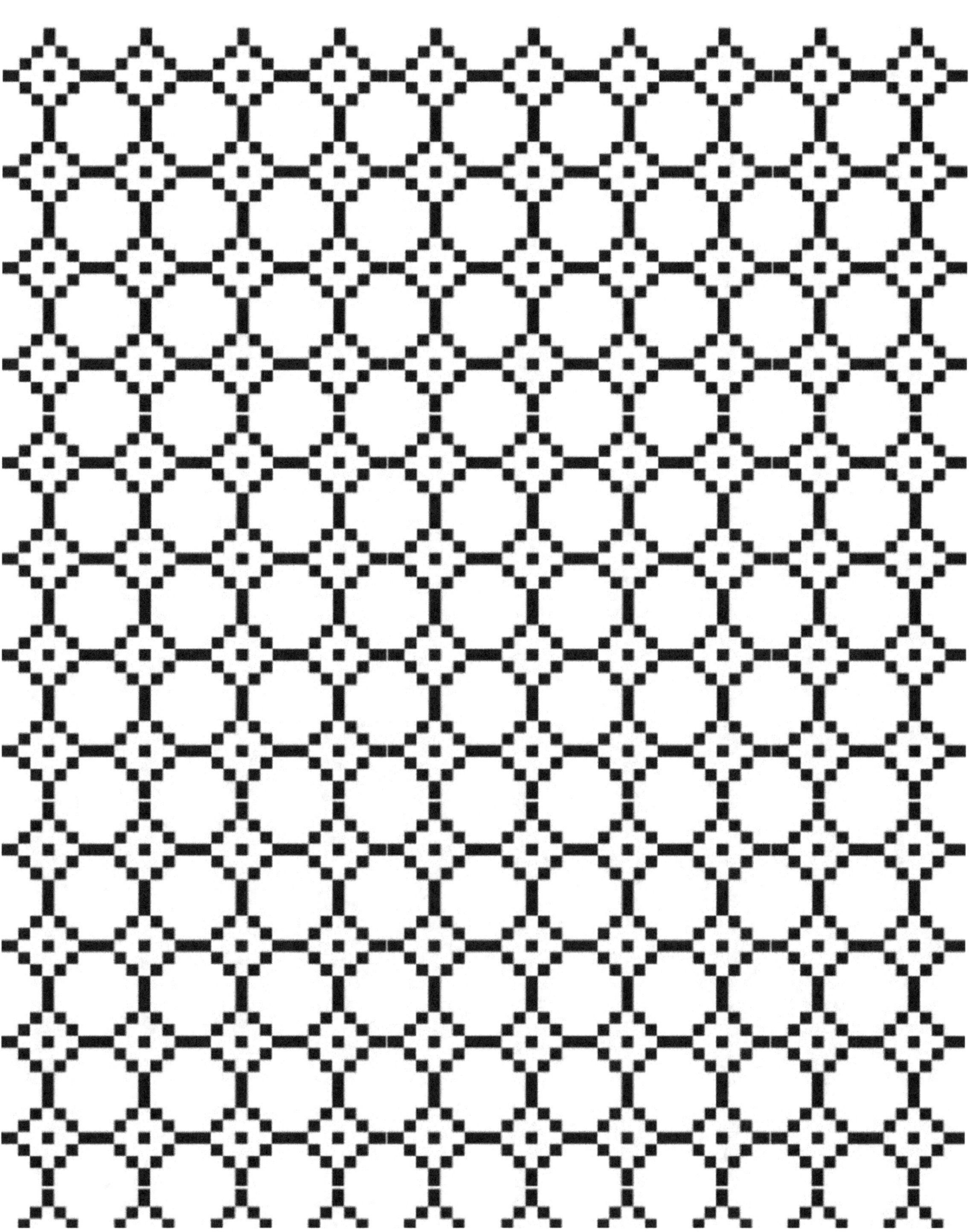

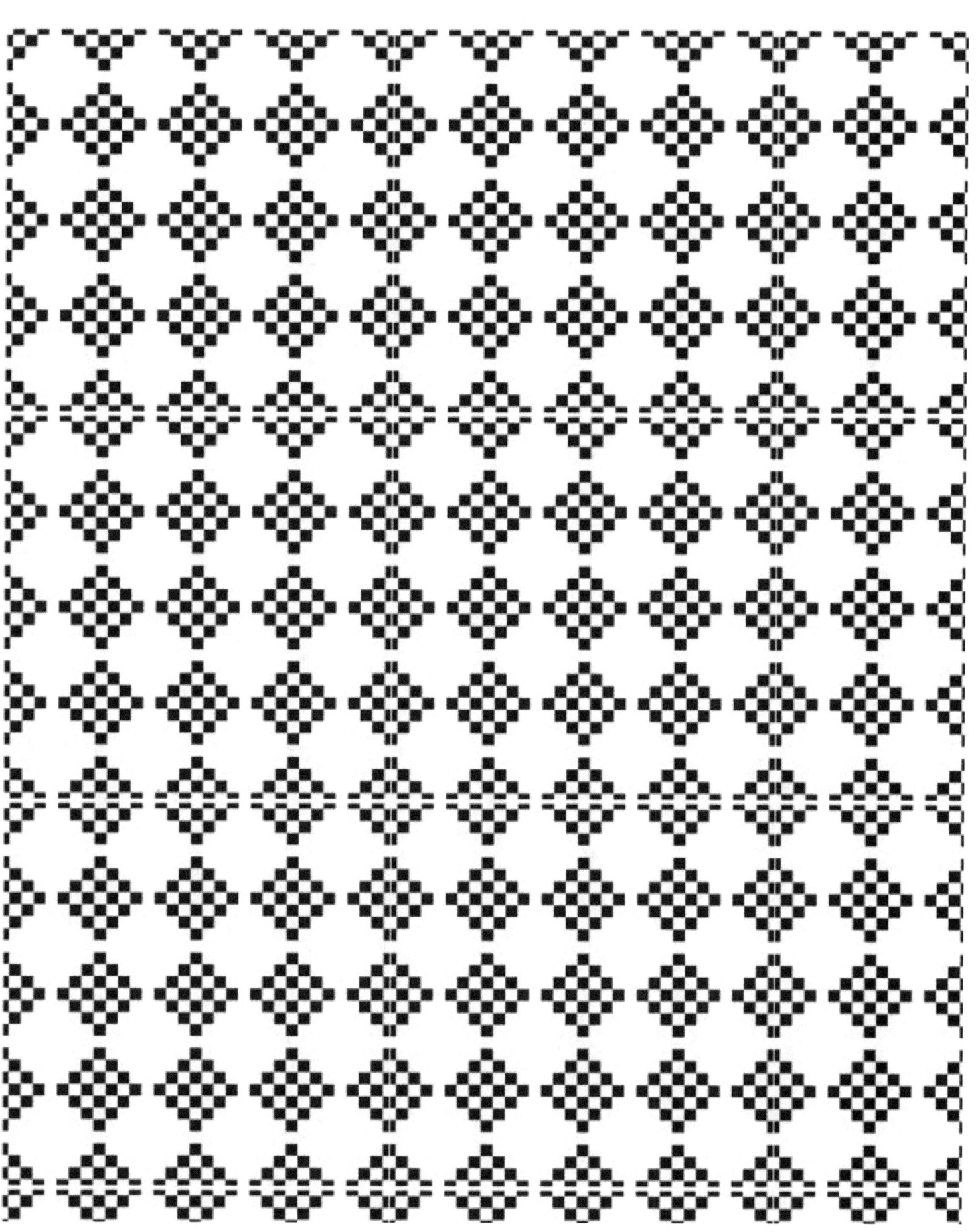

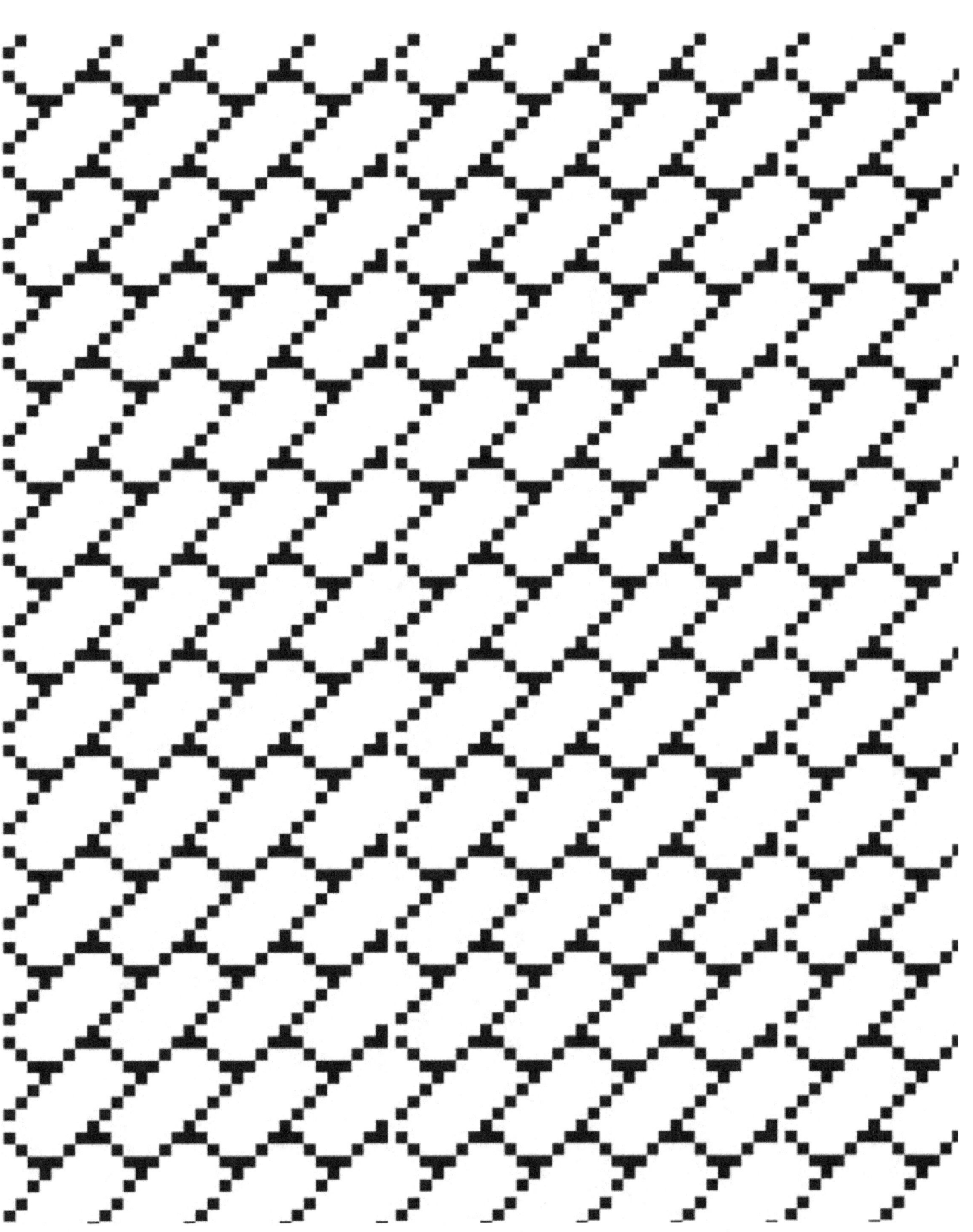

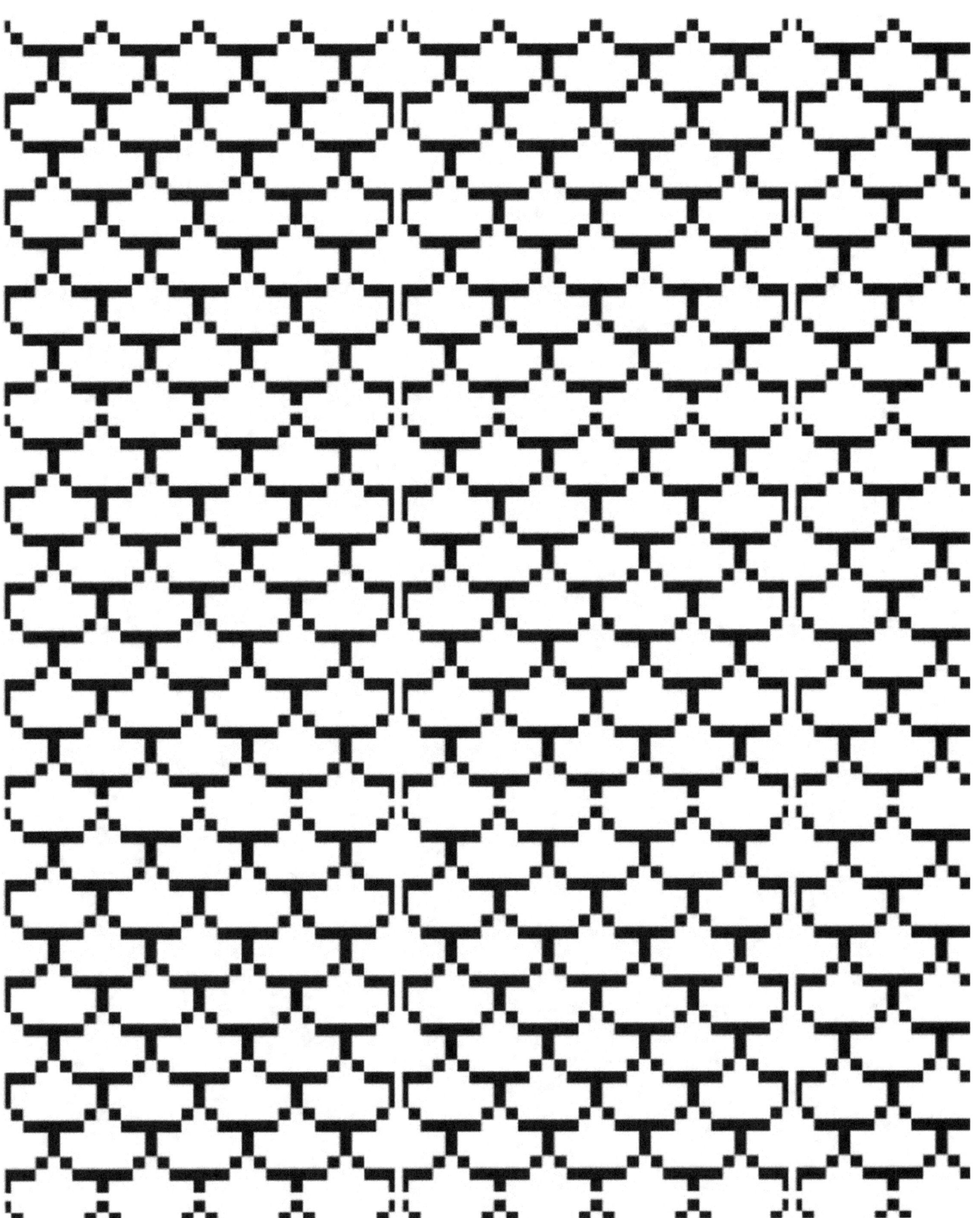

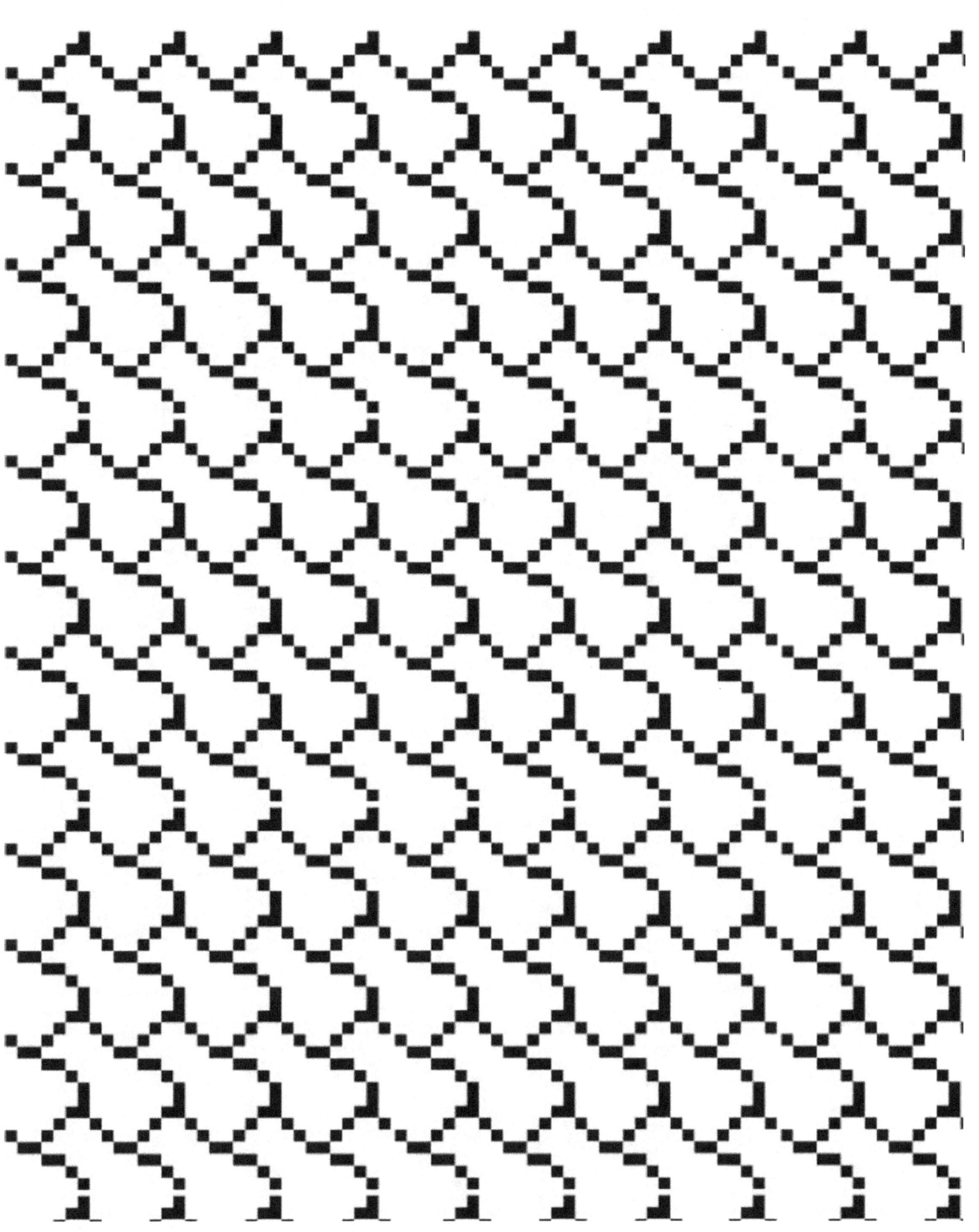

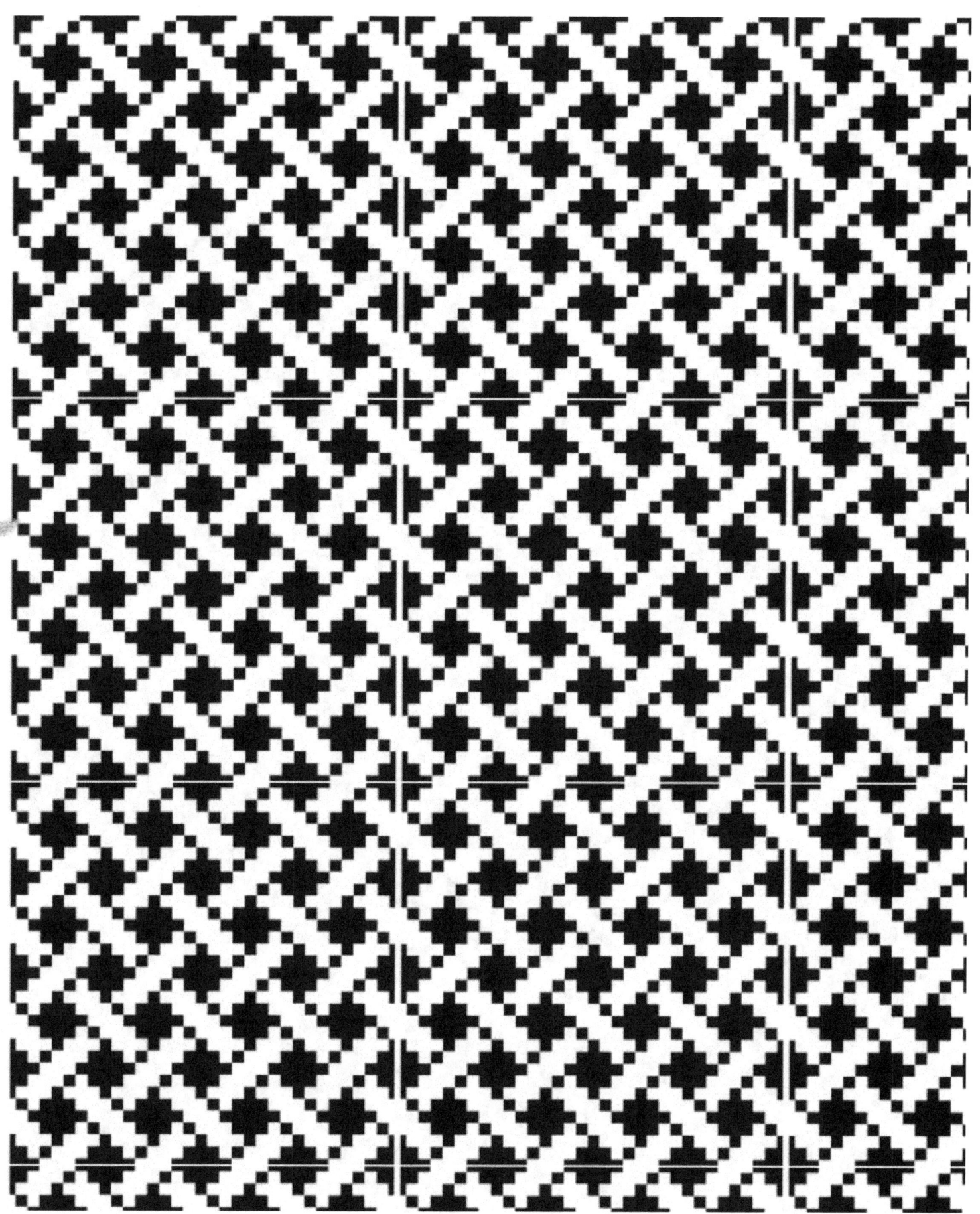

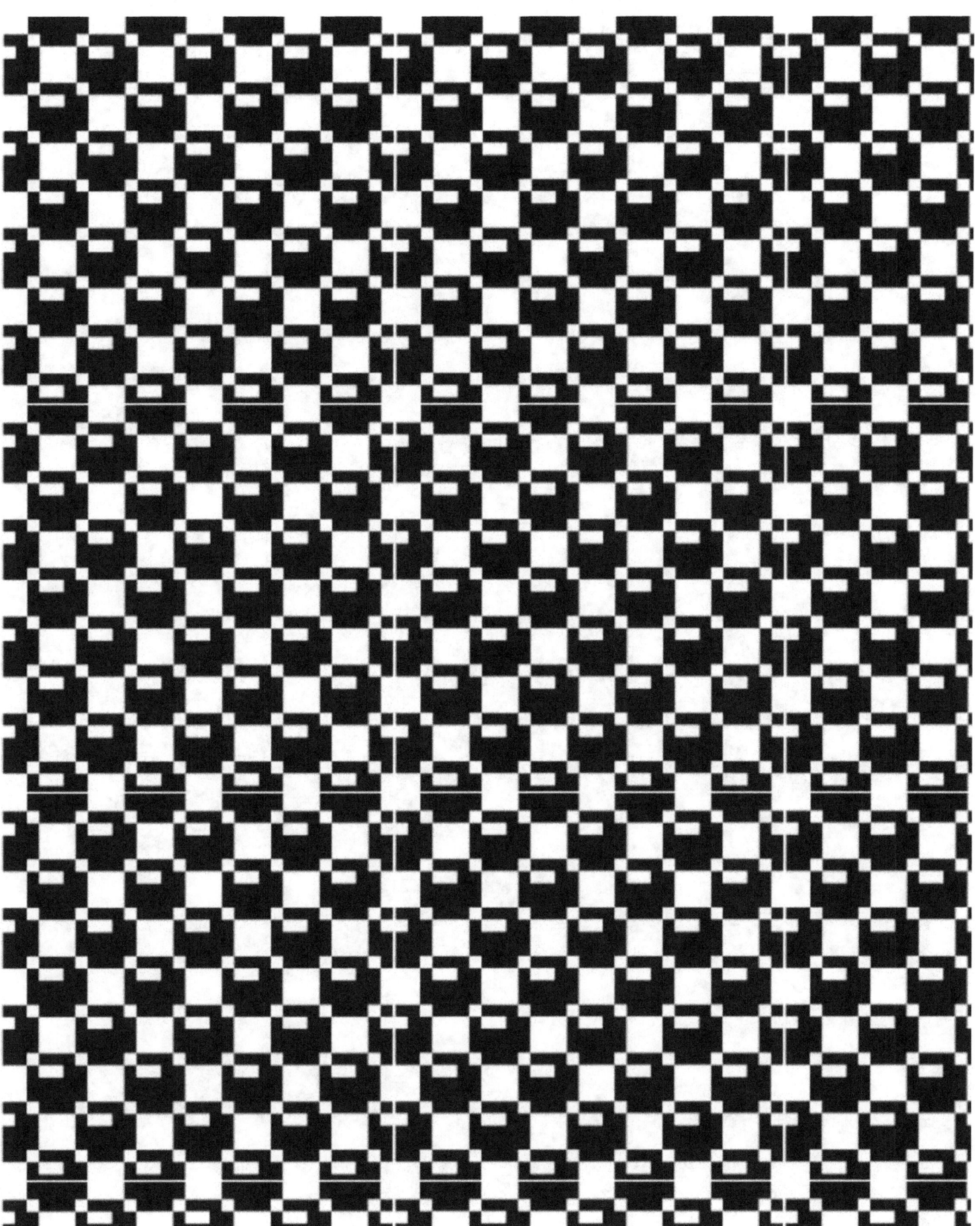

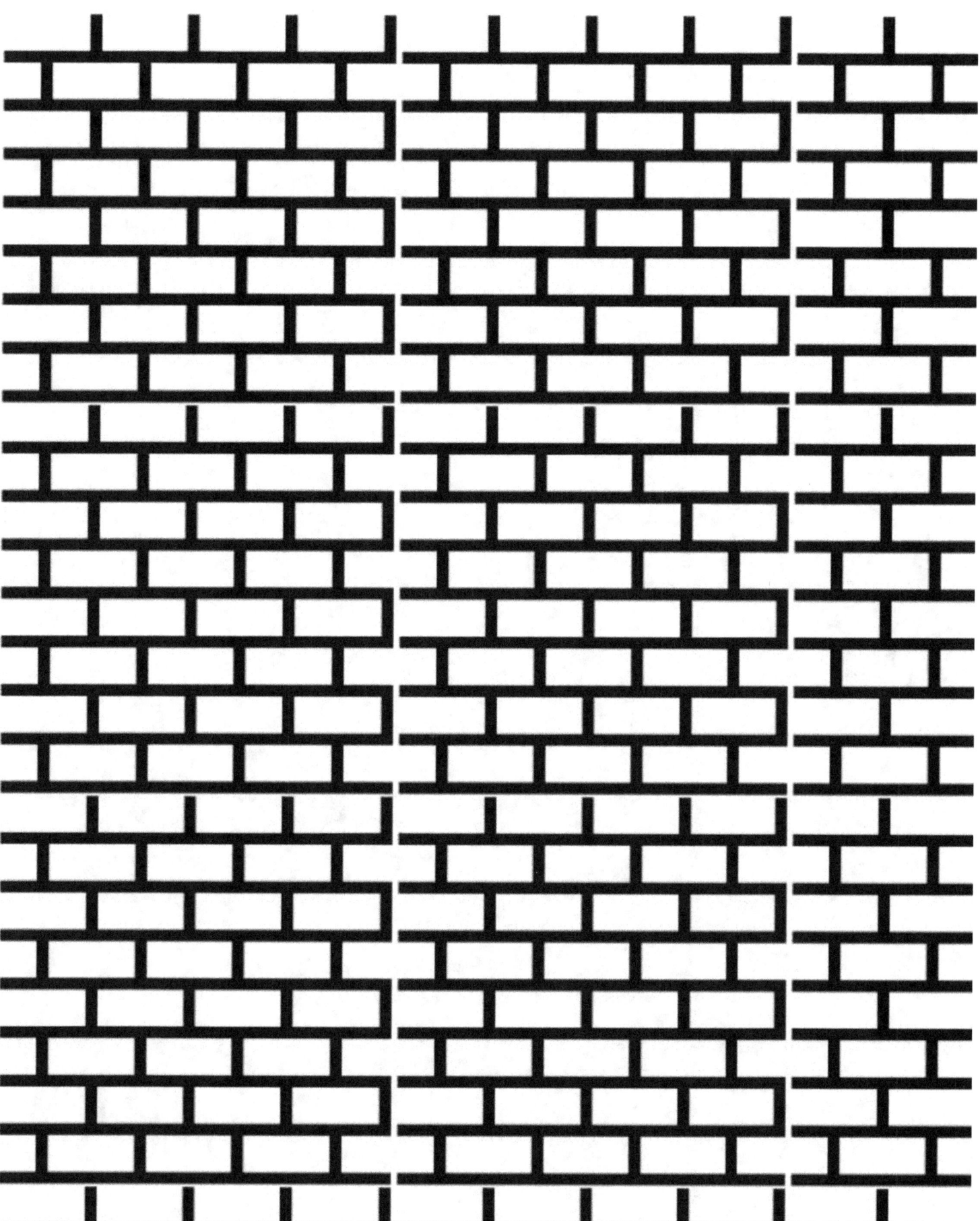

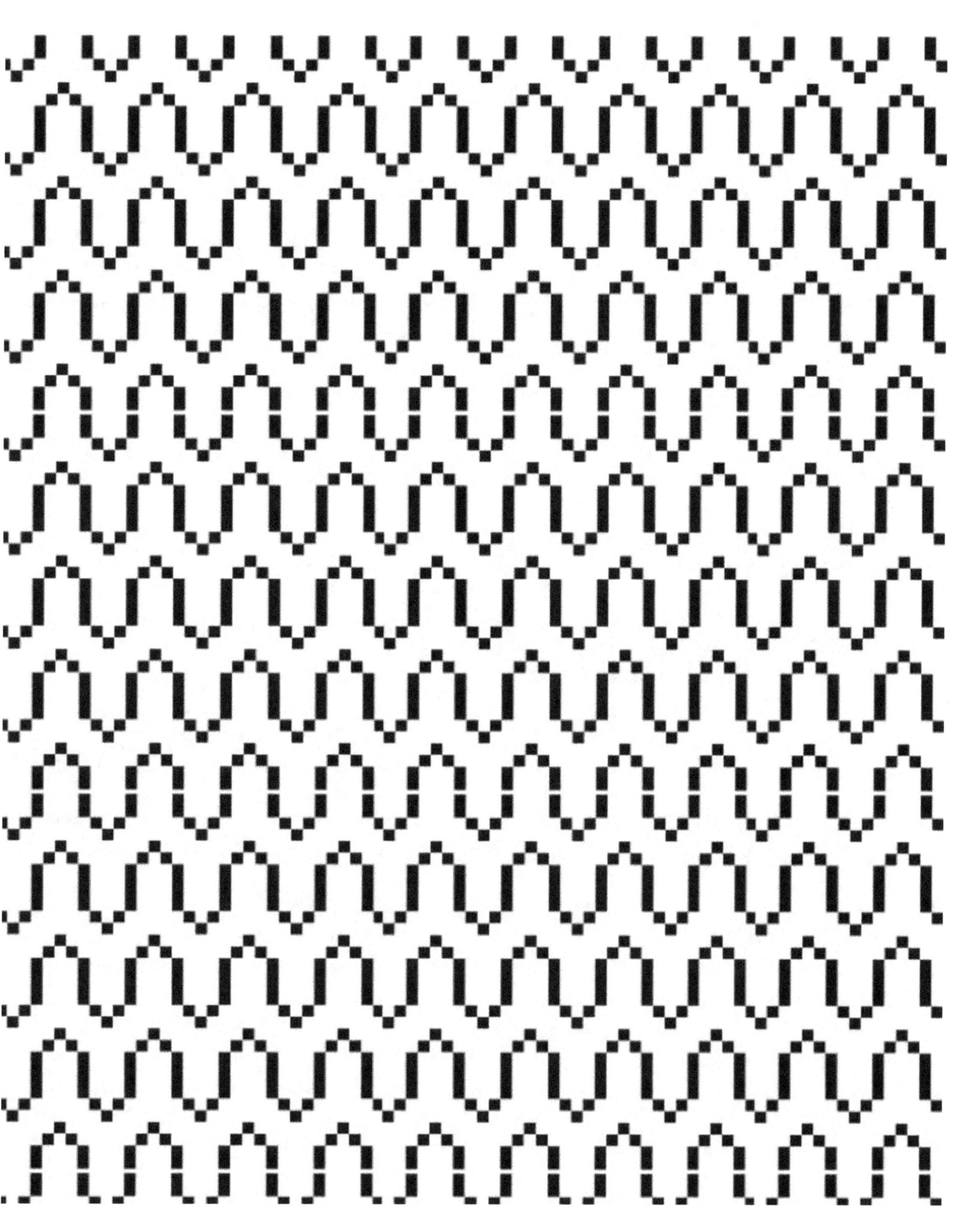

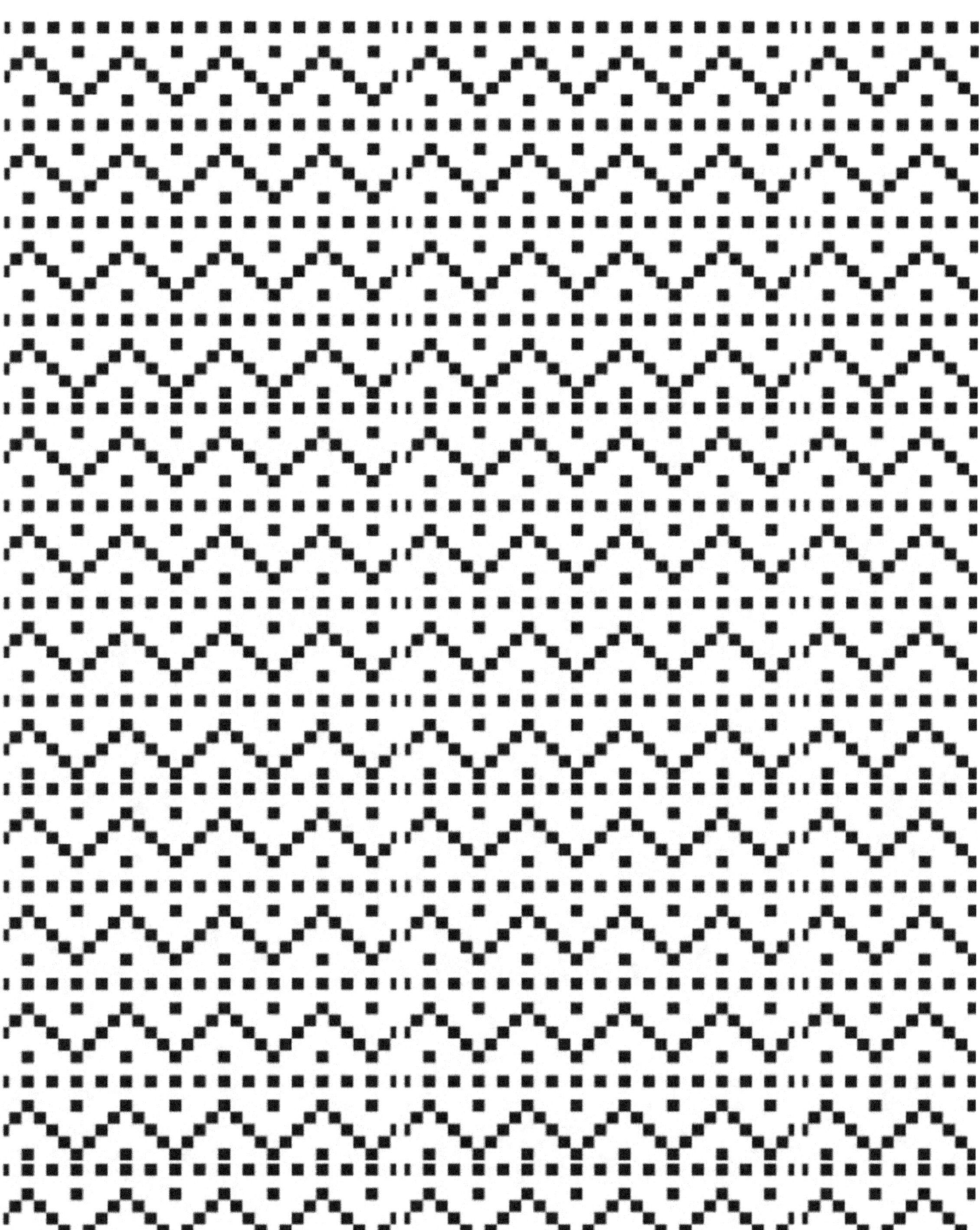

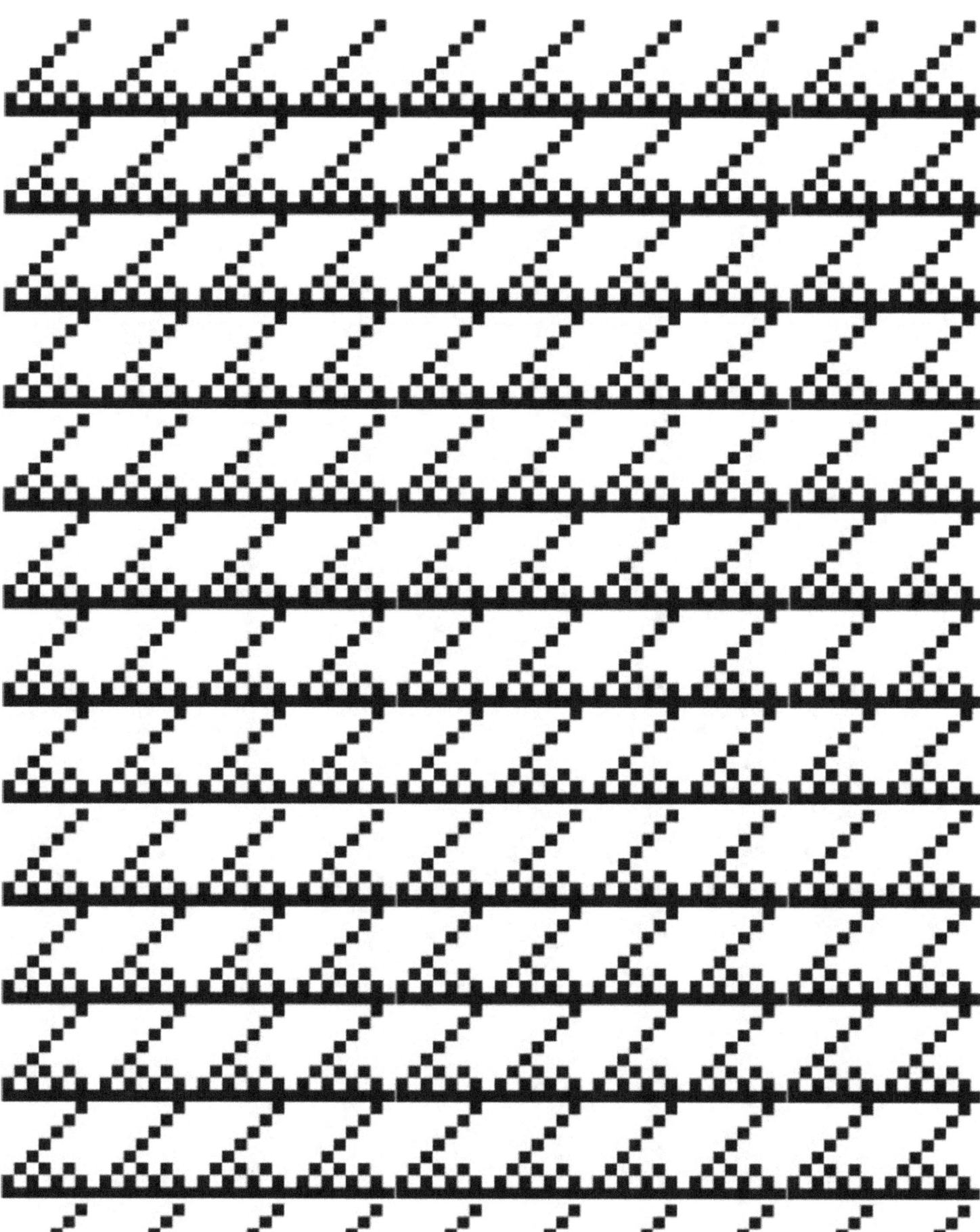

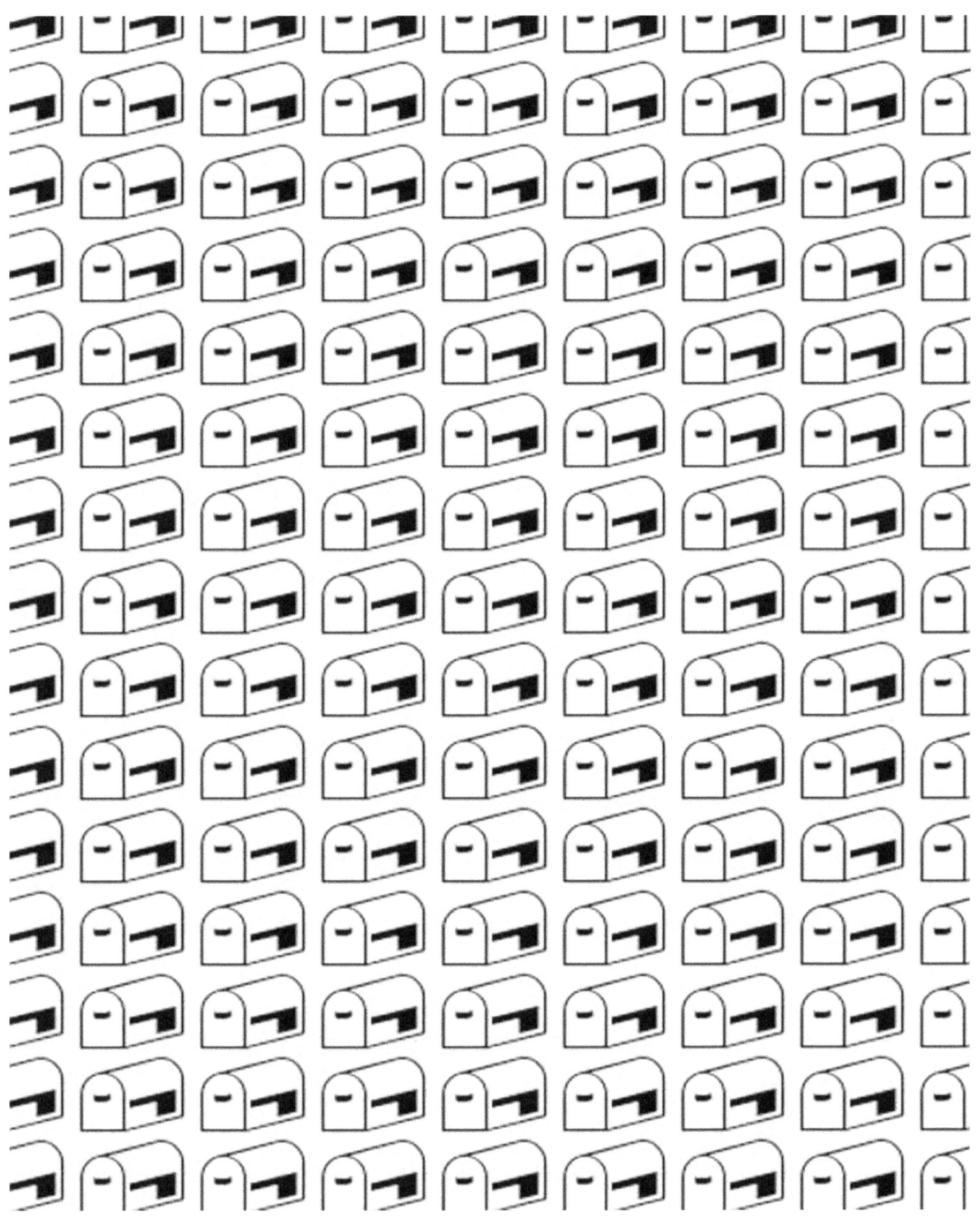

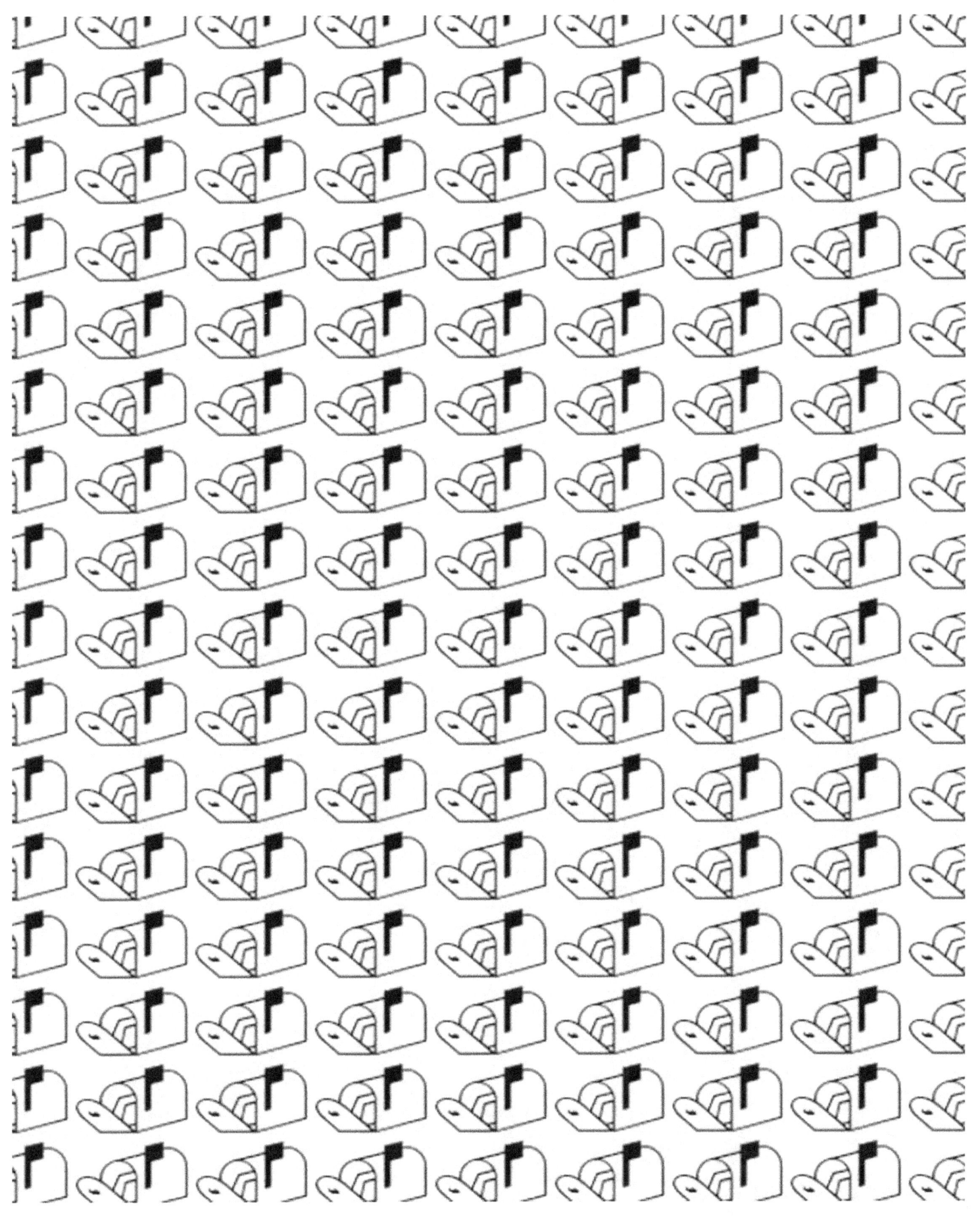

www.ingramcontent.com/pod-product-compliance
Lightning Source LLC
Chambersburg PA
CBHW081743220526
45468CB00008B/2214